cour

les 3 vallées

first edition 2004

written and edited by
Isobel Rostron & Michael Kayson

Qanuk Publishing & Design Ltd
www.snowmole.com

the snowmole guide to **courchevel les 3 vallées**
first edition 2004

published by Qanuk Publishing & Design Ltd
45 Mysore Road London SW11 5RY

printed by Craftprint, Singapore

ISBN 0-9545739-5-1

A catalogue record of this book is available from the British Library.

contents

how to use the guide

How much you enjoy your winter holiday depends on a variety of things. Some you cannot influence - you can't guarantee sunshine, good snow, or your flight landing on time... but most things should be within your control. With the majority of ski holidays lasting just a week or less, you don't want to waste time trying to find a good restaurant, or struggling with an overgrown piste map. The snowmole guides are designed with 2 purposes in mind: to save you time by providing essential information on the operation of the resort, and to help you to make the most of your time by giving insight into every aspect of your stay.

The guide is not intended to be read from cover to cover. After the introduction to the resorts, the guide is split into 4 distinct sections - getting started, the skiing, the resorts and the a-z - so you can dip into the information you need when you need it. Some information will be useful to you beforehand, some while you are in resort and some while you are on the mountain.

getting started   deals with the basics: how to get to the resorts, how to get around once you're there, and your options when buying your lift pass, renting equipment and booking lessons or mountain guides.

the skiing   gives an overview of the mountains and the ski area, information on the off-piste, and a breakdown for beginners, intermediates, experts, boarders and non-skiers. The ski domain has been divided into digestible chunks and for each there is a detailed description of the pistes and lifts.

the resorts   covers the best of the rest of your holiday: for each of the resorts, there is a series of reviews on where to eat and where to play as well as general sections on what to do when skiing isn't an option, facilities for children and tips for seasonnaires.

the a-z   comprises a list of tour operators, a directory of contact details (telephone numbers and website addresses) and information from accidents to weather, a glossary of terms used in this guide and in skiing in general, and an index to help navigate your way around the guide.

how to use the maps

The guide also features a number of maps, designed and produced specifically for snowmole. While the information they contain is as accurate as possible, some omissions have been made for the sake of clarity.

route maps
show the journey to the resort from the UK, from relevant airports or the roads within the area surrounding the resorts.

resort maps
one for each resort (showing pedestrianised zones, main buildings, and where relevant, car parks, train lines, and road names).

ski maps
each individual area has its own contoured map. These show details such as the lifts, pistes and mountain restaurants. The contours have been mapped to fit an A6 page - few ski areas are perfect rectangles. They are accurate only in relation to the pistes they depict and should not be used for navigation. Pistes are shown only in their approximate path - to make the maps as user-friendly as possible some twists and turns have been omitted. The ski maps are grouped together at the back of the book to make them easy to find and refer to - even with gloves on. There is an overview map on the inside back cover that shows the entire ski domain and how the individual ski maps fit together. The back cover has a flap, which is useful as a page marker for the individual ski maps. In the chapter on the skiing the overview map is reproduced in miniature alongside the descriptions of the individual sectors.

explanation of icons

review headers

relevant icons

price rating

☎ 0479 055578

🕔 7:30-10:30am, 4pm-10:30am

✗ traditional savoyarde

map details: page number, grid reference & map cutout showing type and number reference

basic details

- ☎ - telephone number
- 📠 - fax number
- @ - email address
- W^3 - website address
- 🛏 - number of beds
- 🖃 - office address
- 🕔 - opening hours
- ✗ - food type

ski school icons

- ⛷ - ski lessons
- 🏂 - snowboard lessons
- 👨‍👧 - child-specific lessons
- ♿ - disabled skiing
- ⚡ - specialist courses
- **G** - guides available

hotel icons

- 👢 - on-site rental store
- 🚌 - shuttle bus

others

- ✗ - food available
- 🍴➜ - take away
- 🎵 - live music
- 📺 - tv
- 🖱 - internet station(s)
- 🍸 - bar
- • - terrace

town maps

buildings

- *i* - tourist office
- *lp* - lift pass office
- PO - post office
- 🛒 - supermarket
- 🎬 - cinema
- ✝ - church

travel specific

- **P** - parking
- **P̂** - covered parking
- ⓑ - bus stop
- 🚌 - route specific bus stop

commerce colour coding

- ■ - savoyarde restaurant
- ■ - restaurant
- ■ - cafe
- ■ - take-away
- ■ - bar
- ■ - nightclub
- ■ - hotel

route maps

 - train line & station

 - main road & town

 - country borders

 - motorway & town

 - airport

graphic design by
Danek Publishing & Design Ltd

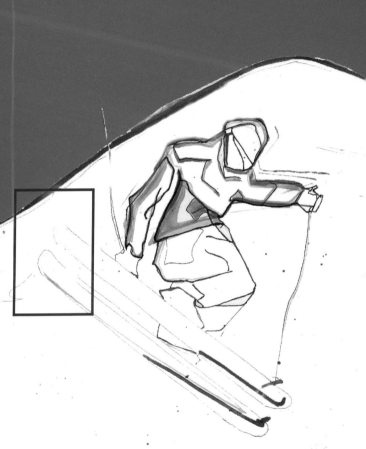

introducing courchevel

courchevel

Ask most skiers to describe Courchevel in one word and most would say "expensive". But there is more to Courchevel than just Euros. First there's the choice of resort: what is known as 'Courchevel' is actually 5 distinct villages. Of these 4 are distinguished by their altitude - 1850, 1650, 1550 and 1350 (also known as Le Praz). The small hamlet of La Tania lying between Le Praz and Méribel is the 5th - considered as one of the Courchevel resorts for the purpose of the lift pass. All lie in the Vallée de St. Bon, one of the valleys in the world-famous Trois Vallées ski area - the other 2 of the Trois are the Vallée des Allues (home to Méribel and Mottaret) and the Vallée de Belleville (Val Thorens and Les

Menuires). After variety, there's the convenience. Courchevel 1850 was the trailblazer for ski in/ski out resorts - a format since copied by many others - with pistes converging at a central point and accommodation built at the edge of the piste. American skiers used to long walks or even car journeys to get to the slopes are amazed by the proximity of piste to bar and bar to bed. Thirdly there's the view. The panorama is of a spectacular massif of jagged and rolling peaks interspersed with the green of pine forests and the blue of glaciers.

Courchevel's clientele is a cosmopolitan mix. 1850 is loved by the jetset and welcomes legions of wealthy and often glamorous French and English skiers and boarders. It is also becoming a destination of choice for Russian wintersports enthusiasts. The clientele of the lower resorts is less definable and can be anything from Dutch families to groups of English 20-somethings.

Accommodation is as diverse as its clientele, ranging from the very best French hotels to the most utilitarian of apartments - defined by where you stay. Many of the streets of 1850 could as well be called Millionaires Row, being lined with palatial chalets and the greatest cluster of 4* hotels in France outside of St. Tropez - there are no 5* only because France doesn't do them. 1650 and 1550 is a mix of more modest chalets and hotels, and some sky-scraping apartment blocks. Le Praz retains many of its original buildings and La Tania is a purpose-built enclave of chocolate box chalets with the odd high-rise thrown in just to remind you you're in France.

While Courchevel's après is not as obvious as that found in some Austrian resorts, there is generally something going on somewhere. 1550 is the quietest village of the 5. In 1650, Le Praz and La Tania, après is concentrated in 1 or 2 places - mainly because there are only a couple of choices in each - so it's easier to find the action than in 1850 with its more numerous hotel bars, pubs and clubs.

11

The widest range of cuisine is also found in 1850 - from Asian to classic French - as is the biggest hit on the wallet. Those staying in the lower resorts will find a more limited choice - typically pizza and Savoyarde food - but prices can be half of what you pay in 1850.

For a long time the 3 Vallées could claim to be biggest ski area in the world - and in piste acreage it was. In 2004, the linkage of Les Arcs to La Plagne by the Vanoise Express cable car brought a young pretender to the throne with the creation of the Paradiski area. Yet

snapshot

highs...
quantity of pistes
quality of lifts
skiing convenience
ideal for beginners
a long skiing day

and lows
as French as fish and chips
muted nightlife
mountain high prices
mayhem during school holidays
3 vallées links susceptible to bad weather

in terms of connections and skiability, the 3 Vallées is still king, and still dwarfs the ski areas of most European and all North American resorts. The name of the ski domain is now a bit of a misnomer as there are actually 4 valleys, thanks to the addition in recent years of lift links and pistes in the Maurienne valley, just over the ridge from Val Thorens. Whatever, the 3 Vallées offers skiing for every standard - but it is predominantly about covering miles and with a total 600kms of pistes if you ski them all you've effectively travelled from London to Manchester and back again, with a warm-up round the M25. The lift system (but not the lift pass system) is one of the most efficient and modern lift systems in the world - and is constantly being up-dated. Though the majority of visitors to Courchevel are happy to stay on the piste there is enough off-piste in the 3 Vallées to justify a book about it - 'Les 3 Vallées Hors pistes - Off piste' by Philippe Baud and Benoit Loucel.

1850 is the biggest and the most famous of the resorts in the St. Bon valley - world renowned for its wealthy feel and Parisian chicness. The spirit of 1850 is perhaps best summed up by the frequency with which small planes land at the miniature airport - the Altiport first welcomed guests by plane in the 1960s and literally established 1850 as a destination for the jet-set. 1850 was the first purpose-built ski-in/ski-out resort - constructed in the mid 1940s on previously undeveloped farm land owned by (local) farmers. Buildings now spread in a lopsided 'v'-shape up the mountain, from the Croisette (1850's rather ugly heart) - on the left (west) side to the Altiport and the areas known as Jardin Alpin and Bellecôte and on the right to the area known as Chenus. If you are looking for glitz and glamour this is the Courchevel for you.

12

Courchevel **1650** (or Moriond) is smaller and more laid back than its higher neighbour. Spaced out along the main road up the valley (that ultimately leads to 1850) its charm is not initially apparent - and thanks to the stark architecture so favoured in the 1970s much of the development hit all the branches of the ugly tree on the way up. But this unpretty façade hides a welcoming atmosphere that 1850 lacks in places. Popular with mid-market UK tour operators, it's a fun and friendly place to spend the week. And 1650 was where downhill skiing in the Courchevel valley started - the first ski lift (the St. Agathe draglift) was constructed here.

The original Courchevel village is **1550** - it kindly let 1650 and 1850 share the name, as long as they distinguished themselves by altitude. Now it is a mish-mash of architectural styles - some remnants of the original buildings remain, but these have largely been overtaken by large blocky apartments. Recent developments such as Le Hameau des Brigues are kinder to the eye.

le praz is Courchevel's museum, where the original buildings and spirit of the St. Bon commune has been best preserved - with its cobbled streets and original buildings the feel is more French and it has the largest year-round population. The heart of the village is found at the small square in front of its 1 hotel (Les Peupliers). As popular as 1650 with UK tour operators, Le Praz's altitude is the only drawback - lying at 1300m skiing home can be impossible at the extremes of the season.

The last of the resorts to develop, **la tania** is a purpose-built hamlet (though this description belies its charm) constructed for the 1992 Albertville Winter Olympics. Set amongst the forest, its safe, self-contained nature makes it is a popular destination for European families.

Predicting the weather in the mountains is always difficult. If you are staying in Le Praz or La Tania, you have to bear in mind that balmy temperatures in the resort can be something much chillier higher up. Unless you're well prepared you can start off warm enough and end up with the shivers in the space of a lift ride.

temperatures

Temperatures are easy to generalise - December and January are usually the coldest months, with things warming up through February, March and April. Don't be fooled by appearances though - it will often be colder when there is a cloudless, blue sky than when snow is falling. Temperatures can range from as low as -10°C in the higher resorts (and colder up the mountain) on the coldest days to as high as 20°C late on in the season when the sun is shining.

13

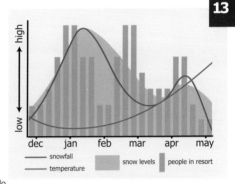

snowfall
temperature
snow levels
people in resort

snowfall

When and how much snow falls varies from year to year, but trends do emerge. Snow levels are quite consistent above 1850, peaking in January and Feburary. At lower altitudes the snow also tends to be at its best during the colder months - melting more quickly as temperatures warm up. Nearly all of the home runs have some help from snow cannons, at the beginning and end of the season and every day in a poor season.

volume of people in resort

As with most European resorts, Christmas and New Year are busy. But while in other places there is a post-New Year lull in early January, Courchevel stays busy with an annual influx of 10,000 Russian skiers and boarders. Then there is a brief respite before the French and English half terms start in February when skiers appear like families of rabbits, meaning long queues, fully booked ski schools and less choice in the ski shops. Being some distance from a major airport, Courchevel is not an obvious choice for weekenders.

Ski resorts are as varied as DNA. But what makes Courchevel Courchevel? To have a quintessential time...

arrive in style

Courchevel 1850's airport has probably the most used airstrip in the Alps. Yet

while other high altitude landing spots are used primarily for accidents and emergencies Courchevel's piece of runway is used for the arrival and departure of guests. Just make sure that your luggage is Louis Vuitton and remember it's not the done thing to turn up with too many bags of duty free.

witness a crime

Can €7 for a hot chocolate be legal? Prices on the mountain and in 1850 confirm the resort's reputation as one of the most expensive ski destinations in France and possibly in Europe. Cries of daylight robbery are as common as orders for a coke and frites.

find some corduroy

Not to make a fashion statement - though that is entirely up to you - but to ski.

It is difficult to imagine more perfectly groomed slopes than those found around the Courchevel resorts. And the piste bashers are clearly proud of them as they publish a map each day showing which pistes were groomed overnight and so where you can expect to find neatly ridged snow - as long as you get there before everybody else does.

go star-gazing

Popular with French and international celebs alike, many world-famous faces from popstars to international sportsmen take their winter holiday in 1850 or even own property there. It's not uncommon to be queuing next to Euan McGregor for the lift, buying your baguette next to the King of Spain or shaking your tush next to Kylie Minogue. As a celeb-sighting is an everyday occurrence in 1850 the done thing is to fix that gaze somewhere else.

take a flexible friend
One of the biggest sports in 1850 is shopping, so much so that the tourist office
publishes a guide to the various commerces. But it's not a place for bargain
hunters - in 1850 we're talking about jewellery and furs, arts and antiques,
designer labels and the latest collections. Gold or platinum preferred.

dance like a cossack
With growing popularity among Russian skiers,
the resort is doing its best to make them feel
at home. The ESF now employs Russian
speaking instructors and the Bergerie
restaurant holds a 'Russian soirée' every Friday
night where you can dine on caviar and wash it
down with the best vodka this side of Moscow.

15

valley hop
In one of the world's biggest ski areas, it would
be rude not to go beyond the limits of the valley. Even beginners shouldn't be
hesitant to pop over the Saulire ridge - the piste from the top of the Col de la
Loze into Méribel is a relatively easy blue track. And while a 3 Vallées lift pass
adds a few extra euros to the bill, your lunch t'other side of the hill will be
significantly cheaper.

indulge in gluttony
From seafood on the slopes (at Cap Horn and
Les Pierres des Plates) to 12 types of foie gras
on 1 menu (Le Bistrot de Praz in Le Praz), the
valley's restaurants are a glutton's paradise.
And for the slothful, the Cap Horn restaurant
will deliver its gourmet options including their
seafood platters (t 0630 528407) to your table.

join the revolution
Not as bloody as some of the ones France has
seen. This one aims to take the fight out of a historically acrimonious business -
getting your ski equipment. Recent years have seen the arrival of a couple of
rental businesses who have an eye on customer service and will come to
wherever you are staying to sort out your equipment. Try Ski Higher in 1850 and
La Tania, or Freeride in 1650.

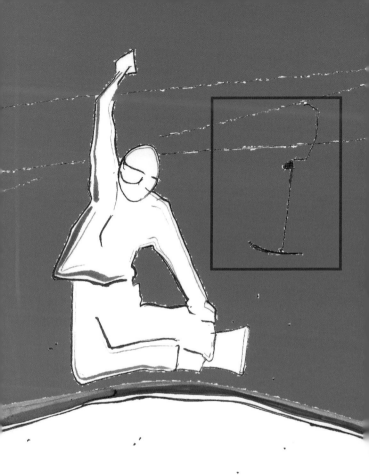

getting started

planning your trip

Once you know you want to go to
Courchevel, you need to decide how
you want to get there. Traditionally,
most skiing holidays are booked though
travel agents or tour operators, but with
the advent of cheap flights, DIY
holidays are becoming more popular.
There are pros and cons to both.

18 package

The theory behind package
holidays is that all you should
have to think about is getting from the
top of the slopes to the bottom. The
core of every package deal is
convenience - though it comes wrapped
in all kinds of paper. Ski companies fall
into 2 types: large mainstream
operators, and smaller more specialist
ones. The mainstream brand offers
ready-made holidays, where everything
is already planned and you take it or
leave it. Trips with smaller companies
can be more expensive, but tend to be
more flexible and many tailor the trip to
your exact requirements. Alternatively, if
you don't want to be restricted to a
single operator, a travel agent will have
access to a selection of holidays offered
by several companies.

Mainstream companies only run week-
long trips, from Saturday to Saturday or
Sunday to Sunday - giving you 6 days
on the slopes and 7 nights in (or on)
the town. They charter their own
flights - making the holiday cheaper -
but you have little option as to when or
from where you travel. Smaller ski

companies give you greater choice -
many specialise in long weekends for
the 'money-rich, time-poor' market, with
departures on Thursday evenings and
returns on Monday evenings. This gives
you 4 days skiing for 2 days off work...
but the real advantage is their use of
scheduled flights, so you can pick the
airport, airline, and when you travel.

With a mainstream company, your
transfer to resort will be by coach, with
others who have booked through the
same company. You may have to wait
for other flights, and on the way there
may be stop-offs in other resorts or at
other accommodation before your own.
Because you're travelling at the weekend
the journey tends to take longer. With a
smaller company you may transfer by
coach, minibus, taxi, or car depending
on how much you've paid and the size
of your group. And if you arrive mid-
week, the transfers tend to be quicker.

What your **accommodation** is depends
entirely on whom you book with. Some
companies only offer apartments, some
specialise in chalets, some operate in
specific resorts... the limiting factor is
what's in the brochure - though if you
want to stay in a particular place, a
more specialist company may try to
organise it for you.

In **resort** some companies offer a drop-
off and pick-up service from the lifts.
But the main benefit of a package
holiday is the resort rep. From the

moment you arrive to the moment you leave, there is someone whose job it is to ensure your holiday goes smoothly... or that's the theory. More than likely your rep will sort out lift passes and equipment rental. Some will organise evening activities and be available for a short period every day to answer questions. Most are supported by an in-situ manager who deals with more serious issues. The more you pay for your holiday, the better your rep should be. The best are service-oriented French speakers... but it is difficult to recruit hard-working, intelligent, bilingual people to work for next to nothing. If you want to know what - or who - to expect, ask when you book.

DIY

If you DIY, you have more control over the kind of holiday you take and what you pay. But as you have to make all the arrangements, you'll need more time to plan the trip.

Several **airports** are within transfer distance of Courchevel - so you can fly to whichever one operates the most convenient flights for you. The major airports are Geneva and Lyon St. Exupéry, which are serviced by the major airlines (BA, Air France or Swiss) as well as some of the budget options (such as Easyjet and bmibaby). Some of the budget airlines also fly to the smaller airports of St. Etienne, Chambéry and Grenoble. The cheapest flights are normally from London, and the earlier

you book the cheaper it will be. The airlines accept reservations for the upcoming winter from around June or July. Some chartered airlines such as Monarch or Thomas Cook may also have a limited number of seats for sale. For **transfers** to Courchevel you have a variety of options (➥ getting there). If you don't want to fly, the excellent European motorway system makes **driving** to the Alps surprisingly easy. Getting there by **train** is also an option.

On a DIY trip the choice of **accommodation** is endless - you are not restricted by brochures or company deals... however the easiest way to book a chalet or an apartment is through a company or website offering accommodation only, such as Interhome or ifyouski.com. You can liaise with the owners directly if you can find their details, but this is often difficult. For hotels you might be able to get a discount off the published price by contacting them directly. For more information on hotels, chalets and apartments ➥ accommodation.

In **resort** is perhaps where the difference between DIY and package is most noticeable. There is no rep on hand so you have to buy your own lift pass, organise your own equipment rental... but this can have its pluses: you can be sure that you get exactly the right type of pass and you can choose which rental shop you use.

How long it takes to get to Courchevel is something of a lottery - the turn-off from the motorway is in Moûtiers, which is also the turn-off for the other resorts in the 3 Vallées and is en route to the Paradiski and Espace Killy ski areas. As such it can be a bit of a slog on transfer day, particularly making your way through Albertville, which needs a bypass road like you need your morning coffee.

20

All contact details for the transport listed can be found in the directory.

over-land
The most common starting place for any journey by **car** to the Alps is Calais. You can reach Calais from the UK via the **eurotunnel** or by **ferry**. Then by car it is just over 670 miles (just over 950 kms) from Calais to Courchevel - a journey that can be done in about 11 hours.

The journey from Calais takes you east of Paris, through Reims to the mustard town of Dijon (about two-thirds of the way if you want to make an overnight stop along the way). From Dijon head down past Bourg-en-Bresse to Lyon where you head east towards Moûtiers and the Courchevel turn-off. There are 2 *péage* (toll) stops on the route south through France - you collect a ticket as you enter the motorway and then pay in cash or by credit card as you leave. Expect to pay around €50 in total.

The French Gendarmerie operate a queuing system on and off the Albertville-Moûtiers section of the motorway at weekends - which although frustrating is quite effective and prevents you from having to rely on your driving survival skills. Although it is only approx 25kms from Moûtiers (Salins Brides Les Bains) to 1850 (and so less to the lower resorts), the winding road up the mountain and the snakey lines of traffic can make it feel longer - especially if there is snow on the road.

There are 2 alternatives to the standard ferry crossing to Calais. The first is with Norfolkline to Dunkirk - often quieter (and less prone to lorry strikes!) than the Calais services. The second is SpeedFerries.com - a new fast ferry service to Boulogne. SpeedFerries sells tickets on a similar basis to the budget airlines - the earlier you buy, the less you pay.

Ski Méribel offers a door-to-door **sleeper coach**, from London and Dover to Moûtiers. Transavoie run a frequent **bus** service from Moûtiers train station to all the resorts in the Courchevel valley. Services run more frequently at weekends. All return journeys must be booked 48 hours in advance at the tourist office. A one-way ticket to 1850 costs €11 (and less to the lower resorts) - children aged between 4 and 12 years travel half-price. The service starts at 6:30am and runs to

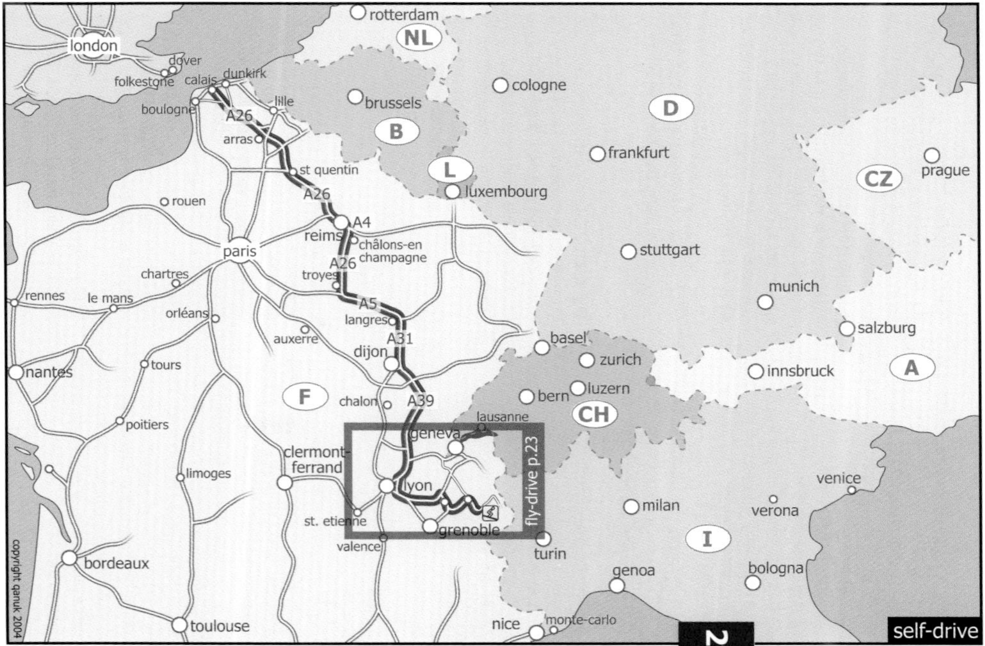

fly-drive p.23

copyright qanuk 2004

midnight on peak days. Transavoie has an office in 1850, just below the Croisette and in the tourist office in 1650. Alternatively a **taxi** from Moûtiers costs about €60.

Travelling by **train** to the Alps gives you more time in resort - 8 days instead of the usual 6 - a particularly excellent service if you live in London. The stop for Courchevel is Moûtiers. All train services from the UK become full months in advance so be sure to book well ahead - tickets are released in the July before the start of the season.

The **snowtrain** is the classic way to travel by train to the Alps. You check in at Dover on Friday afternoon, take a ferry to Calais where you board a couchette (a train with sleeping compartments) and travel overnight, arriving in the Alps on Saturday morning. The return service leaves the following Saturday evening. Another option is the **eurostar overnight** service, which leaves London Waterloo (with some services stopping in Ashford, Kent) on Friday evenings. You travel directly to Paris, where you change onto a couchette to travel overnight, arriving in the Alps on Saturday morning. The return service leaves on Saturday evening. The **eurostar direct** service runs during the daytime, leaving London Waterloo on Saturday mornings and arrives in the Alps on Saturday evenings. The return trip departs on

Saturday evening. If you can't get onto the Eurostar services, the French intercity service (**TGV**) is an option. The journey from Paris (Gare de Lyon or Austerlitz) to Moûtiers takes anything from 5-8 hours. There are a few services every day - some of which are direct, some of which require on 1 changes. To get to Paris, you can either fly or take the Eurostar.

Once you get to Moûtiers you can continue on using the Transavoie bus service or by taxi (as for coach travel).

by air

Courchevel lies within relatively easy reach of 2 international airports - Lyon St. Exupéry (190kms) and Geneva (145kms). There are less frequent air services to St. Etienne (245kms), Grenoble (170kms) and Chambéry (110kms) (➜ planning your trip).

transfers

If you fancy your chances on the French motorways getting to Courchevel by **car** is a viable option. You can hire a car at any of the airports - book over the phone, on the internet, or when you arrive at the airport. Your car will have the necessary equipment such as an emergency triangle, but you will need to specifically ask for snow chains and a roof box if you want them.

The transfer from Geneva to 1850 by road takes an average of 2½ hours (and less to the lower resorts). If you

22

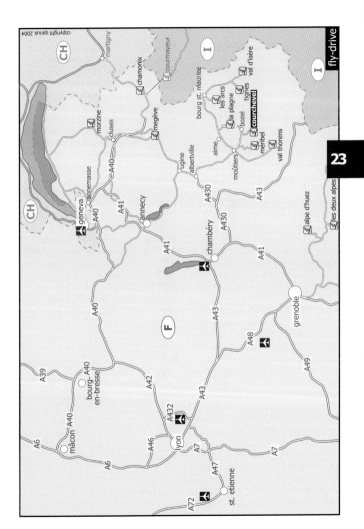

travel at the weekend or during the annual holidays expect traffic and delays - during the peak weeks, journey times can treble. The journey by road from Chambéry takes about 1 hour 20 minutes, and from Lyon 2 hours, though as for Geneva double it (and more) for travel during peak weeks or at weekends.

24

You can get to Moûtiers easily by **train** from Lyon (3 hours), Grenoble (2.5 hours) and Chambéry (1.5 hours) - there is no direct service from Geneva, which makes it a more tiresome option.

Société Touriscar runs a reasonably priced **bus service** from Geneva (€100 return) to Courchevel for the duration of the season. A similar service is run by Transavoie from Chambéry and by Satobus Alpes from Lyon. Seats for all services must be reserved at least 48 hours in advance. If you don't want to drive or take public transport, a number of companies run **private minibus transfers** from the airports direct to your accommodation. Services vary from a simple pick up and drop off to the provision of welcome packs and food and even champagne during your trip. There are a number of services including ATS, Alp Line, Mountain Transfers and Alpine Cab. All of them take online bookings, either via email or direct through the relevant website. ATS run shuttles from Geneva, as well as private transfers. Most of Alp Line's

services run from Geneva though they will pick up from any of the French airports (though this costs more). Mountain Transfers pick up from Geneva, Chambéry and Lyon St. Exupéry and also Moûtiers. Alpine Cab is the luxury option, picking up from Geneva, Grenoble, St. Etienne and Lyon. 3 Vallées transfers is a Courchevel and Méribel specialist offering transfers from the airports and Moûtiers. **taxi** is an expensive alternative - a one-way trip from Chambéry airport costs just over €200 while from Geneva or Lyon it is closer to €300. Or if you really want to splash out you can always take a **helicopter** - it is possible to charter one from all of the international airports through SAF Air Courchevel for up to 5 people. Prices vary according to distance from the resort (not whether you fill it) - from Chambéry €950, from Geneva €1400 and from Lyon €1600.

around & between resorts

Whether or not you use the public transport system in the valley will depend upon where you stay. All of 1650, 1550, La Tania and Le Praz can be covered easily **on foot** with only short walks between accommodation, skiing and après - so unless you decide to explore further you can get away without stepping onto a bus. 1850 is a different story - if you stay near the Altiport you might think the walk down the hill into town is fun but the walk back up is considerable.

2 **bus** services (free with your lift pass) run between 1850, 1650, 1550 and Le Praz 8:30am-midnight - and 1 of these also runs every couple of hours to La Tania. The trip from 1850 to Le Praz takes about 30 minutes. The frequency of each bus depends on the route - though in 1850 and 1650 you'll rarely wait more than 10 minutes - with more services run at the weekends.

taxi is an expensive way to get around and between resorts, but can be an essential means of transport for those staying on the fringes of Courchevel 1850. The directory lists some of the English-speaking taxi drivers operating in Courchevel or alternatively you can ask at the tourist office for a full list.

If you **drive** to resort you can park on some of the roads in the resort - but only where indicated or you could find the local police towing your car away.

---

snapshot
from courchevel 1850 by road to
méribel - 40 minutes
la tania - 10 minutes
val thorens - 1 hour 15 minutes
les menuires - 1 hour
val d'isere - 1 hour 45 minutes
les arcs - 1 hour 25 minutes
la plagne - 1 hour 20 minutes
tignes - 1 hour 45 minutes

25

On some of the less main roads, make sure your car does not get buried under several feet of snow, after over-enthusiastic snow-clearing operations - though at least this gives owners of avalanche kit a reason to use their snow shovel. 1850, 1650 and 1550 have large underground car parks - the first hour's parking is free and then a small charge is payable. When attempting to get around 1850, it's a good idea to work out your route before setting off, otherwise you could find yourself taking a circuitous tour of the village's one-way system.

between valleys

A bus runs between Courchevel and Méribel once a day. As no buses run direct between Courchevel and Val Thorens the options are taxi - a purse-shattering €140 - or a change in Moûtiers.

accommodation

At the end of the day on the slopes, you probably won't mind where you rest your head. But when planning your holiday, you might want to put more thought into where you stay. And with over 30,000 beds in the Courchevel valley, you should be able to find somewhere to unpack your luggage. For luxury accommodation it is hard to beat 1850 - the resort has the greatest number of 4*luxe and 4* hotels anywhere in France, except for St. Tropez. The rest of the resorts have the typical choice of mid-range hotels, chalets and apartments. The 1850 tourist office has a central reservations office (t 0479 0812444, i courchevel-reservation.com) for accommodation bookings - be it hotels, apartments or chalets - in any of the resorts. Packages are also available - which include such things as lift passes and transfers to the resort.

hotels

Courchevel 1850 has 9 4*luxe hotels, 14 4* hotels , 18 3* hotels, 7 2* hotels and 1 1* hotel - and you can expect champagne on the menu at even the 3*s. In France the number of **stars** a hotel has is directly connected to its facilities. Things like room size and whether there is a lift dictate how many stars are awarded. Where the rating system can be misleading is in the divide between 2* and 3*. Often a room in a 3* hotel will not be noticeably different to a much cheaper room in a hotel with 1 less star. Nonetheless the

4* hotels are generally the most comfortable and have the widest range of facilities. The hotel scene in 1650 is about to undergo a renaissance as well with the opening of hotel Le Seizena hotel (under the same management as 1850's excellent 4* *luxe* Kilimanjaro hotel) - though regulars will mourn the demise of the Signal hotel and its very popular mutzig-serving bar. 1850's hotels are spread throughout the resort - with a handful of the centre and the majority along the road up to the Altiport or in the satellite areas of Jardin Alpin or Bellecôte. Higher up what you lose in terms of closeness to the heart of the resort you gain in convenience and easy access to the slopes - your hotel will be either ski in/ski out or the pistes within reach by a short walk. Even some of the hotels in the centre are on the side or a short walk from a piste. Those hotels some distance from the shops in the village have a **rental shop** on site - although the choice may be more limited. And as you would expect with bubbly behind the bar, the overall standard of **facilities** is incredible - saunas, Jacuzzis, swimming pools... pretty much anything your heart could desire.

1650's few hotels are either in or within walking distance of the resort's centre and the main lifts up to the skiing - the same is true of 1550. Le Praz's one delightful offering is on the village square and a short walk from the main lift station.

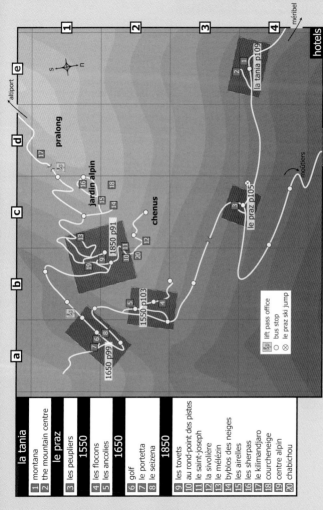

la tania

1 montana
2 the mountain centre

le praz

3 les peupliers

1550

4 les flocons
5 les ancolies

1650

6 golf
7 le portetta
8 le seizena

1850

9 les tovets
10 au rond-point des pistes
11 le saint-joseph
12 la sivolière
13 le mélézin
14 byblos des neiges
15 les airelles
16 les sherpas
17 le kilimandjaro
18 courcheneige
19 centre alpin
20 chabichou

lift pass office
○ bus stop
⊗ le praz ski jump

hotels

la tania p109

le praz p105

1850 p91

1550 p103

1650 p99

pralong

jardin alpin

chenus

méribel

altiport

moûtiers

accommodation

During the peak weeks of Christmas, New Year, and the February half-terms, the hotels will only take week long **bookings**, either Saturday to Saturday or Sunday to Sunday. Outside of these weeks, it is possible to book a shorter stay, although you are more likely to get a long weekend if you book last-minute.

28 Every front-of-house employee will speak **english**, so unless you have a quibble with a cleaning lady you will be able to survive with no French at all. But hotels are where you will notice a difference if you can speak in French. Staff are more likely to be more sympathetic to questions (or complaints) if you make the effort to communicate with them in their language.

prices
The price ranges are approximate figures for a double room per night in high season, including tax but not service.
luxury over €300
mid-range €150-€300
budget under €150
In addition most hotels have low, mid and high season price brackets - and some charge even more for the festive periods of Christmas and New Year. All hotels accept most credit cards.

---

snapshot

for...
cheap & cheerful - les tovets
snowy surrounds - courcheneige
peace & quiet - la sivolière
quiet luxury - kilimandjaro
central luxury - st. joseph
budget central - centre alpin
home from home - au rond-point des pistes
upmost chic - mélézin
food to die for - chabichou
tyrolean feel - les airelles
village charm - les peupliers

<< luxury >>

le mélézin****luxe

☎ 0479 080133
📠 0479 080896
@ lemelezin@amanresorts.com
𝒲³ amanresorts.com
🛏 31 (b&b, ½, full)

The Mélézin is easy to miss - with no sign to advertise its existence and an anonymous frontage. Once inside, the style of the Aman hotel group is unmistakable - though the tinted windows ensure you retain your anonymity. The muted décor gives few clues as to its location - apart from the closeness of the Bellecôte piste, the view of which is particularly enjoyable from the comfortable lounge. Old oak panelling, parquet floors, leather chairs and animal print coverings form the look and the books and chess sets mean it doubles as a library and games room - in a truly sophisticated style. Though all bedrooms are pleasant, bath lovers should ask for a 'Chambre Mélézin' - corner rooms with windowed bathrooms and huge tubs with views onto the pistes.

le kilimandjaro****luxe

☎ 0479 014646
📠 0479 014640
@ welcome@hotelkilimandjaro.com
𝒲³ hotelkilimandjaro.com
🛏 35 (b&b, ½)

In keeping with its name this is one of the highest hotels in the resort - found alongside the beginner's slopes just below the Altiport. From a distance it appears to be a cluster of small chalets - actually connected underground - so you feel remote but have the comforting knowledge that round-the-clock service is close by. And the emphasis at the Kili is very much on service - the staff will co-ordinate every aspect of your stay from ski school bookings to lift pass purchase. This is the only hotel in the resort to offer an outdoor hot-tub - a delight even when the snow is falling - in addition to a delightful swimming pool. Though it is some way from the resort centre, the presence of 2 restaurants - Les Terraces du Coeur d'Or for lunch and gastro cooking at Le Coeur d'Or for dinner - and an on-site rental shop mean your every need can be catered for without much effort from you.

29

le chabichou****

☎ 0479 080055
📠 0479 083358
@ chabi@chabichou-courchevel.com
𝒲³ chabichou-courchevel.com
🛏 40 (b&b, ½)

The white clapboard façade belies the traditional inside of a lovely hotel. Nestled on the side of the piste that leads to the Plantrey chair - and therefore ski-in and ski-out - it is as well located for the centre of town as it is for

accommodation

the skiing. But what sets the Chabi apart from its rivals is the food. Home to the Michelin starred chef Michel Rochedy, the restaurant offers a range of delicious tasting menus, and in some weeks cookery courses for those who want to re-produce the menu at home. Post dinner you and your stomach can relax in the Indian styled Salon Jaipur. And you can work it all off in the Chabiforme spa area, which in addition to having all the usual facilities offers special health weeks.

30

byblos des neiges****luxe

☎ 0479 009800
📞 0479 009801
@ courchevel@byblos.fr
𝒲³ byblos.fr
🛏 66 & 12 suites (b&b, ½, full)

A 'leading hotel of the world', Le Byblos des Neiges is the high altitude sister of the Byblos in St. Tropez. While the sea-side sibling has a colourful frontage typical of Mediterranean climes, the des Neiges version is more eastern in theme. Though the exterior is unprepossessing - sandwiched between the less than pretty Jardin Alpin apartment block - inside is richly decorated with dark wood furniture and jewel-coloured furnishings. And while some hotels skimp on common space the Byblos has plenty - numerous corners with cosy chairs and the leather-lined and icicle-dripping Bayader bar. The food at the in-hotel restaurant (the Lebanese L'Oriental) is eastern like the

décor - and makes a welcome change to Savoyarde specialities.

les airelles****luxe

☎ 0479 003838
📞 0479 003839
@ info@airelles.fr
𝒲³ airelles.fr
🛏 59 (b&b, ½, full)

Once inside Les Airelles (the Bilberries), you may be forgiven for thinking you've been magically transported to Austria's Tyrol. Staff are dressed in lederhosen and the décor is more Austrian kitsch than French chic - though more restraint has been shown in the bedrooms than with the costumes. Otherwise this is a fine hotel, nestled among the trees of the Jardin Alpin and offering excellent facilities which include a fire-warmed lounge, a piano bar and 2 restaurants - La Table du Jardin Alpin, where breakfast, a buffet lunch and dinner is served and the smaller Le Coin Savoyard. On good weather days the hotel benefits from a large south-facing terrace, which can be reached on skis and where lunch and afternoon tea can be taken.

le saint-joseph****luxe

☎ 0479 081616
📞 0479 083838
@ info@lesaintjoseph.com
𝒲³ lesaintjoseph.com
🛏 10 & 3 apartments (b&b, ½)

Le Saint-Joseph is a world of understated elegance - from the discreet entrance on Rue Park City to the opulent feel of the main lounge - and is pleasingly old in appearance. The story of its creation is inscribed above the fireplace in the lounge, which with its polished dark wood and fleur de lys stencilling is reminiscent of a room in an old town house. Bedrooms are comfortable and as luxurious as the lounge, with king size beds big enough to sleep a family and claw-feet baths big enough to swim some lengths. Furnishings are in the old French style - warm reds and golds, antiques and candelabra. For those who cherish privacy with their luxury there are 2 duplex apartments (3 or 4 bedrooms, all en-suite) with plasma screen TVs and a private entrance. The only drawback may be that the Joseph is a better home from home.

<< mid-range >>

le chabichou****

☎ 0479 080055
📞 0479 083358
@ chabi@chabichou-courchevel.com
W³ chabichou-courchevel.com
🛏 40 (b&b, ½)

Directly opposite the Chabichou, au Rond-Point des Pistes is a lovely and friendly family-run hotel. Also ski in and ski out, the centre of the resort is within a 5 minutes. The ground floor is home to a lovely lounge area made cosy by

logfires and archways and the occasional pianist, as well as the windowed breakfast room which offers great views down the valley with your croissant - and you are often joined by the family, who are happy to chat about the resort and the area generally. Bedrooms are charming, with roughly hewn white walls and sweet pictures. Though you won't find out-and-out glamour or too many celebs you will leave with memories of a very pleasant stay.

31

les sherpas***

☎ 0479 080255
📞 0479 080934
@ info@hotel-les-sherpas.com
W³ hotel-les-sherpas.com
🛏 40 (b&b, ½)

Though run under the same management as the 4*luxe Annapurna hotel (located above the Altiport), the Sherpas is very different in style and feel. Set amongst the trees of the Jardin Alpin area, the Bellecôte pistes are just a short walk away. The interior seems inspired by its forest setting, and while the chintzy and floral appearance may be too much for some eyes, somehow it succeeds in creating a cosy, warm atmosphere. As with many of the hotels further out of the resort, it has a pleasant swimming pool, sauna and hammam. The staff are extremely friendly and refreshingly do not embrace the mock formality found in other hotels in the resort.

accommodation

la sivolière★★★★

☎ 0479 080833
📠 0479 080573
@ sivoliere@wanadoo.fr
𝒲³ hotel-la-sivoliere.com
🛏 32 & 5 flats (b&b, ½)

32 Located on the Chenus side of Courchevel, La Sivolière is a charming chalet-style hotel with a quieter vantage point than most. Situated on the edge of the forest that backs onto the Dou de Midi, piste access to the ski area is easy - and without the need for negotiating the masses at the Croisette. The standard of rooms and facilities overall are impressive, and justify the recent upgrade from 3* to 4* status. Some of the newer bedrooms have balconies overlooking the pine trees, fireplaces or a jacuzzi, and there is a bar, 3 lounges and a restaurant so you don't have to make the trek into the resort if your day on the slopes has drained you of all energy.

golf★★★

☎ 0479 009292
📠 0479 081993
@ alex.courchevel@wanadoo.fr
𝒲³ hoteldugolf-courchevel.fr
🛏 46 & 46 apartments (b&b, ½)

More akin to a business hotel than your typical ski resort accommodation, though the Hôtel du Golf is functional it serves its purpose. Occupying a prime location at the foot of the pistes in 1650, it is also right in the heart of the resort. With 47 of rooms it can - and is happy to - accommodate large groups, making it ideal for conferences or corporate trips - there is a meeting room able to take 20 people. Convenience is a recurring theme - within the hotel there is a nequipment rental shop, a restaurant (Le Panoramique), a café with terrace (L'Ours Blanc) and a pub (Le Pub), and underground parking for self-drivers. It can also accommodate disabled skiers with ease.

le portetta★★★

☎ 0479 080147
📠 0479 081623
@ info@portetta.com
𝒲³ portetta.com
🛏 45 (b&b, ½, full)

The slightly Eastern-bloc façade belies the charming interior of the hotel Portetta. Situated next door to the Hôtel du Golf, it has a more individual feel than its neighbour. The large lobby is a sunny room with views onto the bottom of the 1650 pistes and is invitingly laid out with brightly coloured sofas, and a 360 degree open fire circled by a cushion clad bench - or for sunny days you can relax in the slope-side terrace. Despite only having 3 stars to its name, it offers excellent leisure facilities - a swimming pool, a small gym and a pool table, or for the more energetically challenged an in-house masseur and beauty salon.

les ancolies***

☎ 0479 082766
📞 0479 080564
@ message@lesancolies.fr
🌐³ lesancolies.fr
🛏 30 (b&b, ½)

les peupliers***

☎ 0479 084147
📞 0479 084505
@ info@lespeupliers.com
🌐³ lespeupliers.com
🛏 31 (b&b, ½)

One of the 2 hotels in 1550, tucked up a side road at the eastern end of the resort. Though the décor is crying out for a revamp to make it more 21st Century than 1985, the atmosphere is friendly and welcoming - and curiously enough, given the rather dated look there is rather modern wifi internet access. 1550 proper is a (downhill) 10 minute walk, and there is a bus-stop nearby should you fancy a trip to any of the other resorts.

33

Le Praz's only hotel, but you won't be disappointed by the lack of choice. Housed in a traditional stone and wood building, Les Peupliers (or the Poplars) overlooks the small village square - which also serves as the hotel's terrace on sunny days - and lies within a short walk of the gondolas out of the resort which take you up into the skiing in the Courchevel valley. Delightfully furnished throughout, the hotel's restaurant (La Table de Mon Grand Père) has a good reputation and offers a tasty afternoon tea as well as the usual lunch and dinner services - pre and post dinner drinks can be taken in Norby's bar.

les flocons***

☎ 0479 080270
📞 0479 081129
@ courchevel-hotel-flocons.com
🌐³ info@courchevel-hotel-flocons.com
🛏 29 (b&b, ½)

Rather better situated than its nearest rival (Les Ancolies) for both the skiing and the resort centre, Les Flocons occupies a sunny vantage point near the bottom of the 1550 pistes. The large south-facing terrace at the front of the hotel means you can make the most of its aspect. Rooms are basically furnished but clean and warm and many have a view of the slopes, while the rest face down the valley.

montana***

☎ 0479 088008
📞 0479 088001
@ hotel.montana@wanadoo.fr
🌐³ alpazurhotels.com
🛏 71 (b&b, ½)

Like 1650's Hôtel du Golf the hotel Montana is at best functional, doing the job it was designed for but little more. Unlike some of the hotels in the valley you won't delight in the décor or coo

accommodation

over the charm but with its location at the foot of the main piste down into La Tania it is conveniently located for the resort's centre and the skiing. The highlight is the fitness suite - consisting of a swimming pool, sauna and solarium, which is also available to non-residents for a small charge. And should the rather robust après found in the other bars in La Tania prove a little overwhelming, the piano bar is a chilled out haven for more serene leisure time.

34

<< budget >>

courcheneige**

☎ 0479 082059
📱 0479 081179
@ info@courcheneige.com
W³ courcheneige.com
🛏 83 (b&b)

One of Courchevel's larger hotels, the Courcheneige occupies an exceptional site at 1900m on the side of the Bellecôte piste - taking ski-in ski-out to a new art form. With no other developments getting in the way you are pretty much assured a mountain view - the panorama onto the nearby peaks of L'Aiguille du Fruit and further away the Vanoise range is hard to beat. The flipside of excellent snow access is that you are some way from the resort's other facilities - and there's a piste between you and the nearest road. If you don't fancy a lengthy walk, you may

well spend on taxis what you save on accommodation. It's a tough choice.

les tovets**

☎ 0479 080333
📱 0479 081144
@ lestovets@aol.com
W³ courchevel1850.com/lestovets.htm
🛏 27 (b&b, ½)

While the Courcheneige wins the award for best budget mountain view, Les Tovets takes the prize for best budget in the centre. Part of the Rue du Rocher commercial frontage, it is hard to beat for location - the lifts at the Croisette are within stumbling distance and if you have a room at the front you can assess the queues assembling there from the comfort of your bed. It also has more facilities than other hotels in its price and star category with a restaurant and bar, sauna and fitness club - though if nothing on the menu takes your fancy you are spoilt for choice with the rest of the resort all around.

centre alpin

☎ 0479 081142
📱 -
@ ca-courchevel@clubalpin.com
W³ clubalpin.com
🛏 52 beds (b&b, ½)

A rare oasis of low cost in the centre of 1850, the Centre Alpin is run by the Fédération des Club Alpin Français - a mountaineering club established in the 19th Century which offers similar services to the UK's YHA. Preference is given to its members - who qualify for a discount - and though bookings for less than a week are possible, they may say no during the peak weeks. Accommodation is in rooms sleeping 2-5 or dormitories sleeping up to 9, so be prepared to make friends.

the mountain centre

☎ 01202 653456

✆ -

@ info@themountaincentre.com

W³ themountaincentre.com

🛏 72 beds (b&b, ½)

TMC is the best budget accommodation in the valley. A 'backpackers hostel' in the loosest sense of the word it offers modern and clean accommodation in 2 chalet-style buildings. You can stay for as many nights as you wish - availability can be limited during the school holidays, as the centre is ideal for groups of children. From Mondays to Thursdays, the nightly rate is lower than at weekends - weekly rates are also available and lone travellers are welcome. On site facilities include a games rooms, internet access, nightly screenings of current films and for extra you can buy food from the snack shop, arrange for the staff to make you a packed lunch or even cook you a 3-course evening meal.

and the rest

The resort's highest offering is the 4*luxe **annapurna** (t 0479 080460, i annapurna-courchevel.com). If you can't get into the St. Joseph try **le lana** (t 0479 080110, i lelana.com) its sister hotel which offers a similar experience. The Chabichou's nearest rival - in terms of restaurant offering and location - is the **pomme de pin** (t 0479 083688, i pommedepin.com). If the standard at the Kilimandjaro is anything to go on, the new 3* **le seizena** (t 0479 014646, i hotelseizena.com) in 1650 will be worth a look.

35

accommodation

chalets

Chalet holidays cater for those who want to stay in a more relaxed setting, but don't want to fend for themselves. If you choose to stay in a chalet your options are either to book with a tour operator or to hunt out a privately run chalet.

tour operators

Courchevel's popularity as a destination for families makes it a prime location for tour operators, and accordingly almost every tour company in existence offers some kind of holiday to a Courchevel resort. Each of the resorts has chalet accommodation - though whereas elsewhere the choice ranges from the basic and functional to the plush and luxurious, 1850 has more than its fair share of the latter. That said, the typical package is the same as anywhere else - bed, breakfast, afternoon tea and on all but 1 night of your stay an evening meal with wine, and a few added extras at the more luxurious. You will be looked after by at least 1 English chalet host and normally a resort manager. Tour companies will also organise flights and transfers, and some offer discounts for groups booking up an entire chalet. The rule of thumb is that the more you pay, the better you can expect the quality of everything to be. But unless you book the whole place you take pot luck with your fellow guests - it can be a war zone or the beginning of a beautiful new friendship - but at least you know you all like snow.

independents

The high price of property in the valley means there are few independent chalets in 1850 - owners prefer to get value(ish) for money by buying in Le Praz and La Tania where the bulk are found. The tourist office has details for some, or the next best bet for finding them is good old Google.

apartments

Ski apartments are typically compact and bijoux, and those found in the majority of the Courchevel resorts do little to rock the tradition. There is luxury to be found, but most comprise 4 walls and a roof, within which you will generally find somewhere to sleep and somewhere to cook, and maybe a tiny kitchen. 1850 seems largely to have overlooked this type of accommodation but there is plenty to be found lower down, particularly in 1650 and 1550. The list of those available is almost endless - though to ease the process most are listed with rental agencies and if you shop around early enough you will more than likely be able to find something to suit. La Tania could as well be known as Maeva land, such are the size of the apartment blocks run there by the French accommodation company. The tourist office in La Tania publishes a list of the private individuals who rent out apartments in La Tania.

Given the buoyancy of the property market in the valley, there are enough property agents to rival an affluent

London suburb. In 1850 **agence de la loze** (t 0479 081400, i gsi-immobilier.com) will help you track down the elusive self-catering options up there or try **courchevel agence sa** (t 0479 081079, i courchevel-agence.com) for the luxurious end of the market. In 1650 there is **agence 1650** (t 0479 082109, i agence1650.fr) or **immobilière diamant** (t 0479 083807, i immo-diamantcom) - which also has branches in 1850, 1550 and Le Praz. And the Alp-wide **cis immobilier** has branches in 1850 (t 0479 082622, i cis-immobilier.com) and Le Praz (t 0479 010852).

résidences

Résidences are effectively large and well appointed apartment blocks, of which Courchevel has a handful. The newer ones have their own gym, bar, swimming pool and sauna - but they are basically self-catering accommodation with a nice foyer. Like apartments they tend to be available on a Saturday to Saturday basis and house between 2 and 8 people, in 2 or more adjoining rooms which will be kitted out with full kitchen facilities and bed linen - all you need to bring is some food. La Tania has the slightly tired-looking and Eurogroup-run **le christiania** (i eurogroup-vacances.com). For a more luxurious option try the extremely pleasant **les montagnettes** (t 0479 002051, i montagnettes.com) 1650, situated in a quiet spot just below the main road running through the resort.

The **domaine du soleil résidence des brigues** (t 0479 083805) in 1550 is a mid-range development, but offers more modern comfort than the Maeva-run **résidence courchevel 1550** (t 0479 009100, i maeva.com). In 1850 the choice includes the the privately run **belledonne** (t 0479 083165) on Rue des Tovets or the Pierre et Vacances **les chalets du forum** (t 0825 070605, i pierreet vacances.com) by the Forum.

camping

You won't find anywhere to pitch a tent in the winter months, but there is a site in La Tania for caravaners or mobile home owners - water and electricity facilities are available in the resort.

a cheaper option

While Méribel has Brides-les-Bains, at present the Courchevel valley lacks a truly cheaper option that is also convenient for the skiing. The only real way to save on accommodation is to sacrifice on altitude. Below Le Praz is the small hamlet of Saint-Bon home to the hotel Les Allobroges Saint-Bon (t 0479 081015) - the hotel runs a free shuttle to the ski runs. If you can cope with some commuting to the skiing the lower-lying village of Bozel has a small selection of accommodation and a free bus service runs from there to the Courchevel resorts. There are plans afoot to link it to the ski area which hopefully will make this a fuller section in future editions.

37

Once you've arrived in Courchevel and found where you're staying, there are a few things to do before you can get onto the slopes. For many people, long queues and language barriers make this the worst part of the holiday. Starting with lift passes the following pages take you step by step through the process and how to survive it.

38

Despite the up-to-date lift system, the 3 Vallées lift pass is one of the most archaic - leaving the area somewhat in the dark ages compared to other resorts. You need to show your pass at the entry to most lifts on the mountain, which on a cold, windy day can be tiresome. And this will continue to be so, as there are no plans for a hands-free system. The price is high for Europe - for 6 days the change you'll get from a €200 note will only be enough for a croissant. But compare it to the price of the North American resorts or break the cost down per kilometre of piste, and it's a veritable bargain.

courchevel or 3 vallées?

The 3 Vallées pass is the most expensive option - the advantage being that you can then ski the whole of the domain, from Courchevel to Orelle. A 3 Vallées lift pass for 6 days or more also gives you a 1 day lift pass in either the Espace Killy or the Paradiski ski areas. You have to collect a lift pass at the central ticket office of the resort you decide to visit. Within the Courchevel

valley itself, you have a choice of 2 passes - one for the skiing above 1650 (it's easy to leave the area covered by this pass, so be careful), or one for the whole (including La Tania, Le Praz, 1550, 1650 and 1850). Both of these passes are marginally cheaper than 1 for the whole 3 Vallées. Any lift pass allows you to use the bus service that runs around the Courchevel valley for free.

handy to know

Societe des 3 Vallées (S3V, t 0479 082000), the company responsible for running the Courchevel lifts has ticket offices in all of the Courchevel resorts. In 1850 you can **buy** your passes from the Croisette, (Mondays-Fridays 8:45am-5pm, Saturdays 8:45am-7pm and Sundays 8:45am-5:30pm), as well as at the bottom of the Pralong lift on the Bellecôte side of the village (every day 8:45am-4:30pm). In 1650, the main lift pass office is at the top of the escalator that leads up from the resort's main road (8:45am-4:45pm, peak weeks 8:45am-7pm) and there is a small office at the bottom of the 3 Vallées chairlift. The lift pass offices in 1550 (at the bottom of the Grangettes gondola), Le Praz (at the bottom of the Le Praz/Le Forêt gondolas) and La Tania (at the bottom of La Tania gondola) are open 8:45am-4:45pm and until 7pm in peak weeks. If you are travelling with a tour operator they usually collect lift passes for you.

You can buy any pass for any number of days. It is more cost effective to buy a pass valid for all the days you plan to ski, as the overall cost decreases as the number of days increases. So if you plan to ski for 6 days it is cheaper to buy a pass for 6 days than a day pass for each day. If the original pass is for 5 or more days an extra day can be bought at a lower rate than 1 day pass. It also possible to buy a 3 Vallées add-on if the original pass is for 2 or more days.

Passes for the next day can be bought after 3:30pm on the day before you want to ski. **half-day** passes can be bought for the afternoon from 12:30pm - ideal for late risers. Children **under 5s** and adults **over 72s** can use the lift system for free - though they still need to get a lift pass to prove their age. Children aged between **5-13 years** and 'seniors' between **60-72 years** qualify for a discount, on proof of age.

Children's lift passes can also be bought as part of a ski school package.

A number of the lower lying draglifts are free in the Courchevel valley (in 1850 the Bellecôte, Etoiles and Cospillot; in 1650 the Mickey and Belvédère; in 1550 the Roys; in Le Praz the Envolée; and in La Tania the Troïka). The **mini ski pass** is ideal for beginners who have exhausted their use of the free lifts. Available for just the afternoon or 1 day, this gives access to the Ferme, Altiport, Ecureuil and Epicéa draglifts and the Jardin Alpin, Grangettes, Le Praz gondolas. The Grangettes and Jardin Alpin are open in the evening once the ski runs are closed- it costs €6 for one trip and the journey down is free.

A **family** of 2 parents with 2-5 children aged 5-18 years qualify for a family pass (for just the Courchevel valley or the 3 Vallées) - this saves about 20% on individually bought passes, particularly as discounts for children's passes are only available for those aged 13 or under. In certain weeks a family pass for 7 days can be bought for the price of 6 (check on t 0479 081444, i les3vallees.com).

Passes (family or individual, for any length of day) can be ordered online on the S3V website (s3v.com) as long as you can upload any photos required. If you can't, then there is also a **pre-booking service**, either by post or

39

online - which is a good way to avoid the queues or convenient if you are not staying near a lift pass office. You can have your passes delivered to your hotel, arrange to collect them at the Tourist Office, or from a priority line at the lift office itself.

40

The **pedestrian** lift pass gives access to the gondolas and cable cars in the Méribel and Courchevel valleys. Or pedestrians can buy a ticket for a single trip on a the chosen gondola or cable car (the trip down is free). Depending on the snow, the **early season** lift pass is available (normally in the first 2 weeks of the season) - for 6 days this is €100 cheaper than the full price for a normal 6 day pass and gives access to any ski area open. In the last week of the season (again snow dependent), the **spring** ski pass is about €50 cheaper than full price.

The **option pass** is a good choice for those who will spend more than a week in the area. It gives you 12 days of skiing for whenever you decide. The only drawback is that you must go to office that sold you the lift pass to get a valid ticket for the day you want to ski - so not very convenient if you intend to stay in Courchevel for 1 week and Méribel for another. However, if you plan to visit Courchevel or the 3 Vallées several times during the season, a **season pass** can be the most cost-effective approach.

You need a **photo** for lift passes over 3 days or more. You can buy additional **insurance** when you get your lift pass - for a small extra charge on top of the lift pass price. Known as **carré neige** (t 0479 311080, i carreneige.com) this covers all costs of search, rescue, ambulance and reimburses you for lift passes over 3 days (accident, loss, theft, serious illness or bad weather) and lessons (over 3 days), medical expenses, legal aid insurance, interruption of ski lift service (over 1 day).

skis, boots & boards

There has been a renaissance in the previously hassle-tastic ordeal of getting your equipment sorted. A number of the rental shops will come to your accommodation to kit you out - and it is far preferable to wait in the comfort of your own chalet rather than the stuffy and stressful surrounds of a equipment shop. In the shops Saturday afternoons and Sunday mornings are still the busiest time to get equipment. Unlike over in the Méribel valley all of the resorts have at least 1 good rental shop - so you don't need to travel up to 1850 to get the equipment you want.

handy to know

Getting the **right equipment** will ensure you fully enjoy your holiday. Your feet will hurt if you don't get well-fitting boots so don't be embarrassed to persevere until you find a pair that fits. If they cause you problems on the slopes take them back - all the shops will help you find a more suitable pair. Unless you know you want a specific type or make of ski, take the advice of the ski fitter. They are the experts and will know which is the best ski for you based on your ability and age.

It being France there is the usual range of well-known French snowsport chains - such as Ski Set, Intersport and Twinner. One reason to go to a particular shop is if your hotel or tour operator has arranged a rental deal with them - you may get a cheaper rate or insurance thrown in for free, so it's

worth checking. Most shops stock a varied range of the latest ski equipment from all the usual manufacturers - Salomon, Atomic, Rossignol and Dynastar - but you will have to search a little harder if you're looking for Völkl or Fischer. And because there are so many places to hire equipment, prices are competitive. Equipment for children is often available at a reduced rate - price is normally worked out on the basis of height rather than age. If you are in the market for your own pair of skis, many of the shops will let you test them before you buy. An advantage of buying from a chain is that some provide free equipment servicing.

At most shops you can take out **insurance** (except on test skis) to cover accidental breakage, loss or theft - though skiing on roads is not insurable. Unfortunately skis do get stolen or taken by accident - with so many people skiing on similar skis it's easy for confusion to arise. When you stop for lunch or après it's a good idea to swap one of your skis with a friend so you both have a mis-matched pair. This helps to ensure that nobody will pick up your skis, either by mistake or otherwise.

for skis

In 1850 the leader of the new wave pack is **ski higher**. A British run equipment business, it brings the shop to you - and it's about the only place in

41

41

the resort you can buy a Dakine backpack. It also has a smaller branch in La Tania.

In 1650 **freeride** runs a shop along similar lines. On its website (i freeride.fr), you can reserve rental skis and boots before your arrival, guaranteeing you the equipment you want and saving time. They also offer a mobile service and will deliver and fit equipment in the comfort of your own accommodation, and collect it at the end of your stay.

42

for boots

freeride is also the choice for boots - their staff attend an intensive training session before the season starts. And if you want to buy, in-soles are made to measure - so they should be as comfortable as ski boots get.

For a more continental approach, Bernard in **couttet sports** near to the hotel Les Tovets has a reputation as an good boot-fitter.

for boards

For better boards and more knowledgeable service, go to a specialist boarding shop where the people serving you are more likely to be boarders.

Snowboard specialists since 1988, and it shows... the staff at **snow coco** in 1850are knowledgable as well as

friendly. Don't be deterred by the small interior - it has an excellent range of most types of boards, which are well maintained and serviced.

s'no limit (i snolimit.com) next to Le Jump is also well regarded, stocking a variety of makes of board and board - flow bindings are also available, and for those wanting to buy it has a test centre. There is also a branch in 1650.

prends ta luge et tire toi in 1850 is possibly more concerned about looking the part than in the angle of your binding. That said, the range of kit on sale is impressive and the on-site café with its huge TV screens playing MTV and extreme sport videos make it a pleasant place to browse.

for other equipment

Rental shops offer a lot more than just skis and boards. Most stock a wide range of ski clothing - though brands differ from shop to shop - and all the accessories you can think of, though there is little difference from what you would pay for the same clothes in the UK. The best selection of telemark or touring skis can be found at **le camp de base** (t 0479 080991, i lecampdebase.org), on the ground floor of the Forum. They also stock an excellent range of technical clothing such as Mammut and an assortment of climbing gear. Most places have snowblades, avalanche transceivers and snowshoes.

Ski instructors have trained in the Courchevel valley since the 1920s, when a canny local realised its potential as a destination for skiers. As in most French resorts, the red-jacketed ESF is omnipresent, but here it faces strong competition from some up and coming smaller schools, many of which are specifically focussed on the English market. An advantage of taking lessons is that ski schools have priority in lift queues.

handy to know

group lessons are the cheapest way to learn to ski. When you book you will be asked your level of skiing/boarding ability, either by the colour of piste you are comfortable on, the number of weeks you have skied before, or by the vague 'beginner/intermediate/advanced' pigeonholes. In practice the divisions aren't as accurate as they could be - some people overestimate their ability or misunderstand words like 'confident' and 'controlled', so to and extent the level of your group is pot luck. If you are honest about your skill level you are likely to find yourself (vaguely) in the right place. Group lessons are available for a half or full day - half days are typically 2.5 or 3 hours

If you have the money, **private lessons** are without question the way forward. Once you're past the basics, individual attention is the best way to significantly improve your technique and is often better value. If you can get a

group of four or more the individual price per day is similar to the average price per day for group lessons, with the advantage that you go where you want to go and practise what you want to practise. The length of private lessons varies from school to school, but generally the divisions are simply for a half day (morning or afternoon) or a full day. A half day will be 3 hours of instruction on one side of lunch - though in low season you may be able to have a shorter lesson.

43

prices are pretty standard across the board - though you may pay a little more for the smaller companies, there's not much in it. If you book group lessons you can have a week's worth of half-day instruction for only a little more than it costs to rent your skis. Private lessons (and guides) are a different story, but again you won't find too much variation in what the different schools charge.

Only the ESF and Ski Academy offer lessons for **children** outside of the school holidays. All other schools only provide them over the Christmas period, during most of February and Easter. The schools will generally put children over 13 years old in the adult classes.

There is a specialist **boarding** school, and most of the schools offer some form of surfing lessons. The skill divisions, prices, times and overall format is much the same as with skiing.

prices are generally competitive for all lesson types - though none include ski pass, equipment or insurance.

Either make your **booking** before you get to Courchevel - by email, fax or phone - or once you're in resort, in person at the ski school office. Always pre-book in peak season, as there are not enough instructors to meet demand - and for the half-term you should book some months before you arrive to ensure you get what you want. To confirm your booking, the schools will need your name, level of ability and a credit card number.

44

In 1850 the **meeting point** for most of the schools (except New Gen) is the Croisette - though it could be easier said than done to find your instructor when that's what everybody else there at 9am is doing. In the smaller resorts, meeting points are pretty obvious. No matter where you're staying you won't have to go far - the snow front of each resort functions as the main rendezvous, unless you arrange something different when you book. For the next day's lesson the meeting place will be decided the day before - so pay attention in class - depending upon snow conditions and the make-up of the group. At the end of your lesson you're on your own.

It is illegal to teach in France without a qualification recognised by the French establishment. In effect this means that the majority of **instructors** in France are French, as few other 'international' qualifications are accepted and the equivalence race test that foreign instructors must pass is extremely difficult. But this approach gives you the advantage of knowing that your instructor is at the least a very competent skier or boarder.

There are increasingly more English instructors, even at the ESF - who maintain that nearly all of their non-English instructors speak English. If you hire an instructor for a whole day, it is customary for you to buy them lunch - whether or not you tip is up to you. Almost all instructors speak good **english** and there are also instructors who speak every other language - though you will need to book a long way in advance should you want instruction in a language less common to the Alps.

Lessons take place **whatever the weather**, unless the entire lift system is closed in which case the schools will refund the full lesson price or give you a letter for your insurance company. They will also refund you if you are ill or have an accident and can produce a valid medical certificate. Some of the schools have quite onerous cancellation policies - so don't expect a full refund if you don't give them sufficient notice.

esf (1850)

☎ 0479 080772
📞 0479 081459
@ ski@esfcourchevel.com
W³ esfnet.com
🗐 croisette

The French leviathan has a dominating presence over the ski school market in Courchevel - and in some weeks it can be difficult to see the snow on the Croisette under the sea of red jackets. It is the oldest ski school in the Alps, and becoming an instructor is a difficult enough process that you are guaranteed a quality skier as your teacher. What you are not guaranteed is that you will be taught the latest techniques. Older instructors who themselves learned on older skis may not be entirely up to speed on carving or 'new school' techniques - it has been said that there are as many ways to ski as there are ESF instructors. On the other side of the coin, many of the younger instructors teach both skiing and snowboarding, and there are charismatic and competent teachers in abundance. Each of the resorts has its own ESF office (and its own contact details) - and each school has slightly different strengths and lesson programmes. As you'd expect, the branch in 1850 is able to offer the full range of lessons (including for skwal and big foot if the demand is high enough) and can cater for disabled skiers. The 1650 school (t 0479 082608, i esfcourchevel1650.com, based at the top of the escalator and open 8:30am-6pm) offers every lesson type except group lessons for cross-country. 1550 (t 0479 082107, i esf-courchevel.com, office next to the tourist office) has the best reputation for children (and a meeting point for English customers at the Crosiette in 1850) closely followed by La Tania (t 0479 088039, i esf-latania.com), which prides itself on a open-minded approach to English instructors - in that it actually has some. There is also a branch in Le Praz (t 0479 081459), which offers the standard programme.

45

supreme ski & snowboard

☎ 0479 082787
📞 0479 083173
@ info@supremeski.com
W³ supremeski.com
🗐 rue des verdons

Promoted as *the* British school in Courchevel, many of Supreme's instructors are in fact Scottish, so you shouldn't have too many problems understanding their English... Pre-book your lessons in the UK and you get a 10% discount (except in high season). The school offers the usual as well as daily improvement workshops every weekday afternoon for carving or mogul technique and afternoon snowboard tasters. You can also organise your equipment rental through the school - again if you prebook in the UK you qualify for a discount.

lessons & guiding

ski academy

☎ 0479 081199
🖷 0479 083939
@ courchevel@ski-academy.com
W³ ski-academy.com
🖃 porte de courchevel

46

1850 is the main branch of this French run but English focussed ski school - there is also a small branch in Méribel. Most of the instructors are English and group lessons take a maximum of 8, meaning you'll certainly get more attention than with the ESF. In addition, Ski Academy run children's lessons outside of the school holidays - most of the other schools don't. Though they don't run group snowboarding lessons, surfers (and skiers) can join one of the snowsports clinics - 2½ days of tuition with video feedback.

new generation (1650)

☎ 0479 010318
🖷 0479 004388
@ info@skinewgen.com
W³ skinewgen.com
🖃 freeride

New Generation or "NewGen" is another of the British offerings - its main office is in 1650 (in the Freeride shop) and it has a meeting point in 1850 just below the Croisette. Established 6 years ago all of its instructors speak English - most are BASI qualified, though some are French -

and if you have a group lesson they will guarantee that your instructor is English. family private, 3 hours, €225 - 4 members, off-piste private (instructors with more off-piste training), intro to avalanche, transceivers etc. BASI courses, GAP courses, race training. very friendly, English reception.

and the rest

bass (british alpine ski & snowboard school, t 0479 083387, i britishskischool.com) offer tuition in small groups, while **snoworks** (t 08701 225549, i snoworks.co.uk) offers a programme of courses (all-terrain, bumps, off-piste) for improving skiers that run during various weeks of the season. **magic in motion** (t 0479 010181, i magicinmotion.co.uk) have a small presence in the valley - though their lurid ski suits make them hard to miss. For boarders, **rtm** (t 0615 485904 (fr); 079 8998 8774 (bookings); 077 9953 5746 (enquiries)) is an independent school run by Brits who offer group lessons for surfers for 3 hours every day except Saturdays and Wednesdays - they are qualified to go off-piste.

By far the best - and safest - way to make the most of the off-piste is to hire a qualified mountain guide. As they have spent years getting to know and understand the mountain terrain, not only will they find the best powder but you can trust them to look after your security. The difference between **guides and instructors** is fundamental - instructing is about 'how' and guiding is about 'where'. Ski instructors are not permitted to take you off-piste and you should not ask them to. In contrast the limiting factor with a guide is your own ability. If you are competent enough they will take you anywhere you want to go. There is no question of a guide's ability. Becoming one takes years and requires an intimate knowledge of everything the mountains have to offer particularly how to be safe in this notoriously unpredictable environment. Guides are not just expert skiers, first and foremost they are mountaineers: physically fit individuals, with extensive experience of mountain rescue, practice and procedure. They are also proficient rock and ice climbers and are competent and comfortable in all types of conditions. During the course of qualifying, they are tested on alpine technique, avalanche rescue and first aid, to name but a few. The very definition of a safe pair of hands.

Courchevel's Bureau des Guides (t 0479 010366, i guidescourchevel.com) is based in 1850 on the bottom level of the Forum. Through them you can book a variety of excursions - from off-piste skiing, glacier skiing, ski touring and heliskiing in Italy as part of a group lesson or on a private basis. Price depends upon the size of the group, the activity and the duration. Generally the bigger your group, the less you pay individually. Their guides will also show you around the pistes - but don't expect them to be too excited about doing it. You can also book a guide through the **ski prestige** ski school (t 0479 221117, i skiprestige.com) and the ESF.

If you decide to hire a guide, don't underestimate how fit you need to be to get the most out of the experience. Whilst the guide will cater the day to the standard of the least able skier in the group, he may still lead you along some tiring traverses or climbs to reach the best snow.

47

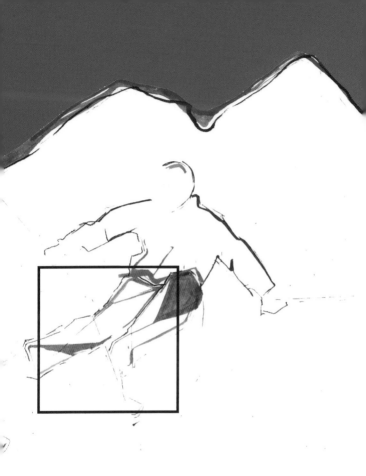

the skiing

The attraction of the 3 Vallées is obvious even on paper - a vast and varied terrain of wide runs, gulleys, mogul runs and forest paths reached easily by an abundance of high-tech lifts. And Courchevel's mainly northerly aspect helps to ensure that that the snow is consistently better than in the other valleys - the skiing in this area can be fully enjoyed from early December until the end of April. Though the slopes are blessed with the early morning sun - so the ice softens earlier in the day than on the south-facing slopes of Méribel or Val Thorens - they fall into shade as early as 3pm in the winter months and 4pm in early spring and so by the middle of the afternoon the skiing can be cold. Conditions aside, the area offers a wide gamut of skiing options - from long, groomed pistes and open bowls to tree-lined slopes and couloirs.

50

pistes

In most resorts, there are times when you stop halfway down a piste, wondering who was responsible for calling it a red when it clearly ought to be a black - or a blue. This experience, however, is very unlikely to happen in Courchevel. The pistes are well rated, well signposted and well maintained - the snow being treated with the same care given to greens on a golf course. Further, each morning the Courchevel lift company circulates a map of the pistes in the Courchevel valley they have groomed overnight - so you know

snapshot

courchevel
150kms of pistes - 31 green, 41 blues, 40 reds, 12 blacks
67 lifts - 1 cable car, 10 gondolas, 18 chairlifts, 38 draglifts
off-piste - 28kms of itinerary routes, numerous couloirs
highest point 2738m
4 snowparks

3 vallées
600kms of pistes - 68 green, 104 blue, 110 red, 35 black
189 lifts - 36 gondolas, 68 chairlifts, 80 draglifts, 2 cable cars, 3 funitels
off-piste - something for everyone: couloirs, trees, powder bowls
highest point 3200m
8 snowparks

where to find the corduroy. On the back you will find a forecast for the day. Links between the different valleys are displayed on yellow boards - confusing for those used to itinerary routes being marked in yellow. Otherwise the piste system adopts the same colour-coding used in all European resorts (➥ 'pistes' in the glossary) but this should only be used as a general guide. Although the gradient or width of each individual piste stays the same, other features such as snow conditions can change daily. Personal feelings about pistes vary greatly - an easy blue to one skier can seem like a vertical drop to another.

off-piste

The resort does not include itinerary routes on its official piste map, and so our descriptions of the 'off-piste' include any routes (recognised or otherwise) that are not groomed or checked at the end of the day. If you intend to venture away from the markers it is best to do so in the company of a mountain guide. As you would expect within such a huge ski area, you will find plenty of ungroomed snow alongside and in between pistes on which to practise your technique without going too far.

lifts

Like the pistes, the lifts are named (on the mountain and on the official piste map). On the whole the quality and quantity of lifts is good with a total capacity of 240,000 skiers per hour. The main bottleneck is at the Croisette in 1850 which sees queues worthy of the M25 during the rush hour for most of the day. Though the queuing system has some way to go to compare to the American or Canadian resorts, it is better organised than some. The ski schools often have a priority queue and some lifts have a quick queue for single skiers and/or families. On some lifts, children under a certain height must be accompanied. Most lifts open in early December - and the remainder by Christmas - and run until the middle or end of April. The exact date changes yearly and if the snow conditions are good, the lifts may open earlier or close later than advertised. The lifts in the 3

Vallées open earlier and close later than lifts in other resorts, giving you the longest skiing day - in the second half of the season, some lifts don't close until 5pm. Opening and closing times are noted at the bottom of each lift and on the official piste map. Wherever you ski - particularly if you cross over into one of the other valleys - it is a good idea to work out which will be the last lift you will take to return home and check what time it closes.

the areas

In the this guide, the 3 Vallées is divided into 11 sectors which are arranged in sequence on the overview map (➥ inside back cover flap) from the Courchevel valley in the east to the Belleville valley in the west. The Courchevel valley is divided into 3 sectors (maps a-c), as is the Méribel valley (maps d-f) while the Belleville valley is divided into 5 sectors (maps g-k). In this chapter you'll find a description of how to get to and from the slopes, the general characteristics and aspect of the area, and detail of the pistes, the off-piste, the mountain restaurants and the local après for each area. The Courchevel valley is described first, then the Méribel valley and finally the Belleville valley:

courchevel

1850 (map b)

1650 (map a)

la tania, le praz & 1550 (map c)

méribel

saulire (map d)

overview

tougnète (map e)
mont du vallon (map f)
belleville
st. martin de belleville (map g)
les menuires (map h)
le masse (map i)
val thorens & maurienne (map j & k)
At the back of the book there is a more detailed table of lift information and a ski map for each area (the piste colours correspond to those used by the resort).

52 coming & going

Where you start depends on where you're staying. Each of the Courchevel resorts has a main gondola from its village up the mountain. If you are staying in one of the lower resorts and would rather work your way up by road, you catch a bus from each of Le Praz, La Tania, 1550 and 1650 to the Croisette in 1850 from where the area's main lifts (but also the main queues) start. An advantage of staying in one of the lower resorts is that you will generally have a more leisurely start to the day than those caught in the chaos around the Croisette. And as the main lift out of each resort is a gondola, you can get up and down the mountain by lift. For those who drive to 1850's main lift station, there is a huge pay & display car park underneath the Croisette, which is rarely full even in peak weeks.

beginners

It is difficult to imagine a more ideal place to learn than the 3 Vallées - though Val d'Isère would argue for joint first place. Each of the Courchevel resorts has a designated nursery slope area and at least 1 free lift on the gentle slopes near to the village. A word of warning though, if you put on skis for the first time in the 3 Vallées, anywhere else may disappoint - the skiing is easy to access and you can often ski to the door at the end of the day. Courchevel 1650 in particular is a good place to start, not least because you can buy a pass just for the 1650 ski area, which helps keep costs down. If you are having lessons, check with your ski school whether or not you will need a lift pass extending beyond this area. Above 1850 there are zones suitable for 'novices' near the Altiport.

intermediates

It is also arguable that there is no better ski area for intermediates - with a seemingly never-ending network of well-groomed runs. Even those with a real mission to ski the whole area are unlikely to do so in a week. If the lift system is fully functional, you won't run out of things to ski. Pick any point on most of the mountain and you can choose between blue, red or black depending upon how up for it you (and your legs) are feeling, or how much wine you've indulged in the night before.

experts

While the 3 Vallées is rarely talked about in the same hallowed terms as Chamonix, experts skiers will find some

52

runs of interest. When all links are open the world is your oyster, and if you know where to look there is plenty of steep and scary. In Courchevel the infamous couloirs may send some scuttling back to the nearby reds while over in Méribel the Face (the site of the 1992 Olympic women's downhill) is always fun. If strong winds or unfriendly conditions keep the higher lifts closed, don't feel frustrated that you can't get high - the old racing runs of Jockeys and Jean-Blanc start lower down the mountain so you can normally get to them whatever the weather. As the bulk of Courchevel's clientele falls into the intermediate category, the expert terrain is often ignored and can be enjoyed in relative isolation. To explore the lesser known off-piste the best advice is to hire a guide - none of the itinerary routes are marked on the official piste map.

boarders

The 3 Vallées offers the same joys for boarders as it does for skiers. Some of the links between areas are narrow paths - which requires a bit of concentration - and the section near the top of the Chenus gondola is annoyingly flat for skiers and boarders alike. Elsewhere (with the odd flat exception, such as the Ours and Truite pistes in Mottaret), you can't go too wrong. On the flipside, most of the main links are by chairlift or gondola, and even where there is a button lift, there is also normally an alternative for the

pomaphobic. And you won't find a t-bar in the whole ski area.

Though there are supposedly 4 snowparks in the Courchevel valley - the best of which is found underneath the Plantrey chair - boarders looking to get some air or practise their tricks may be better off in the Méribel valley. This is home to the Moonpark de L'Arpasson above Méribel and the Plattières snowpark above Mottaret, both of which are generally better composed and maintained.

non-skiers

As a non-skier, the main reason to go up the mountain is to admire the views. The 3 Vallées is very much about skiing and does not cater so well for those reluctant to strap planks to their feet. The designated footpaths are along the flatter pistes or away from them altogether so you don't have to worry too much about being knocked over by an out-of-control skier. With a lift pass (➥ lift passes) you can go up in any of the gondolas or cable cars, but not the chairs or button lifts for obvious reasons. In the Courchevel valley there are about 20kms of walking trails that are groomed all winter long, from strolls through the villages and forests to half-day hikes. Some trails are marked and maintained but they are not supervised - further information on where they are can be obtained from the tourist office.

courchevel 1850

The skyline above the 1850 resort is dominated by the jagged Saulire peak, also the ridge line between the Courchevel valley and the Méribel valley. The top is reached by a trip on the Saulire cable car - a good way to get a perspective on the gradient on the runs underneath. The pistes from the top run down towards the 1850 resort and towards the lift links to the skiing above 1650 (➥ 1650). The descent towards 1850 isn't for beginners as it's straight into some fairly serious skiing - a dazzling choice of reds and blacks all with a great bird's eye view of the much-used Courchevel Altiport and the whole valley below. Here too will you find the start of the infamous rock-encased Courchevel couloirs, only one of which is a piste, Le Grand Couloir. Lower down, as the mountainside falls away in a concave shape, the pistes become more forgiving, changing in grading to blue and green. With Courchevel's perfectionism for grooming pistes, if you catch the first lift up you can ski them at their smoothest.

access

There are 3 lifts from the Crosiette. The Jardin Alpin gondola, which rises up the Bellecôte side of the resort, is generally used during the day by beginners to reach the nursery slopes at the Altiport and later on in the day by skiers returning to their hotels and chalets in the Jardin Alpin area. The Verdons gondola takes you to the bottom of the

map b

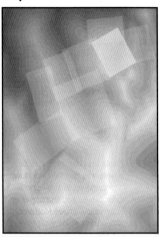

snapshot

out of interest
highest point - 2738m
aspect - n
pistes - rolling greens, connecting blues, long and lovely reds & testing blacks
off-piste - the couloirs, the creux bowl & lots of piste-side patches
restaurants - 6

highlights & hotspots
your wallet
the infamous couloirs
courchevel's snowpark
views of take-offs and landings at the altiport

54

spirit and could easily be classified as green. Beginners will enjoy them on the basis that they are officially harder than a green while intermediates and above will use them for little more than getting to more interesting rus.

From Saulire the runs are a mix of **reds** and blacks. The right fork at the top takes you down the long Creux and Marmottes reds which run down to the crossroads of lifts to 1850 in one direction and 1650 in the other. To the left the long Combe Saulire and Pylônes pistes under the shadow of the Saulire peak run down to the bottom of the Saulire cable car. Along the way you can watch the more advanced - or foolhardy - descending the Courchevel couloirs.

55

Vizelle gondola and the Saulire cable car, from where you can ski back down to the village or go up to the ridge between Courchevel and the upper end of the Méribel valley, above Mottaret. The Chenus gondola leads west from the resort to the slopes above La Tania and Le Praz and to the bottom of the Col de la Loze lift - the link to the top of the ridge between the lower end of the Méribel valley and the Courchevel valley. During peak weeks the queues at the Croisette can be off-putting - a quicker way up the mountain from 1850 can be on the Plantrey chairlift, which ends at Loze.

pistes

All of the pistes below the bottom of the Saulire cable car are **green** - pleasant, gentle slopes through the forest which all merge at the Croisette.

The **blues** are little to get excited about - they are blue in colour rather than

Courchevel's most infamous **black** is the Grand Couloir. Reached from the top of the Saulire cable car, the most daunting part of the experience is the approach - a traverse along a narrow ridge. Once there, the descent is similar to the nearby Suisses black run - both are covered in moguls, although the Couloir, as befits its name, is narrower, but shorter. The Suisses often offers 4 seasons in 1 dayscent - ice, moguls, powder and perfectly groomed snow.

snowpark

According to the official piste map, there are 4 in this valley. Of them, the one by the Epicéa buttonlift is the best defined, with a short boardercross course, 2 pipes (1 easy, 1 less so) and a number of jumps, tables and rails. The remaining 3 are found under the Pralong chairlift, the Biollay chairlift and the Verdons gondola and form part of the pistes - they are not sectioned off from them. They consist of little more than rolling hills (and the one under the Verdons gondola is known as the "flying carpet"), which can come as something of a surprise to beginners who think that they are on a green.

56 off-piste

The obvious choices for off-piste lovers are the 2 ungroomed couloirs accessed from the top of the Saulire cable car - the one on the left as you look up to the peak is known as Télépherique while the next along is named after Emilie Allais. The attraction of couloir skiing is the challenge of getting your turns in where needed rather than the quality of the snow - and for many its a relief to get to the bottom without getting too friendly with a rock on the way down. The forest below the bottom of the Lac Bleu draglift is one place to go when visibility is poor - but beware the tree holes and the risk of avalanche (they are often seen hurtling down the steep sides of Saulire). The bowl from the top of the Creux Noirs chairlift down towards the Creux red run is often skied, but again avalanches are a regular occurrence.

eating & drinking

In a nutshell, lunch in this area is about table-service and high prices. And make sure you reserve in advance.

Situated just above the Altiport, **cap horn** (t 0479 083310) offers sumptuous dining on the mountain. The huge terrace is warmed by gas heaters and the pleasant aspect tempts you off (the) piste. Inside the theme is nautical and cosy with a number of fireplaces, small rooms, tables at different levels and decorated throughout with a blend of wood and stone. Food ranges from the sublime to the ridiculously expensive seafood platter for 2 at €110. And should you be sadistically inclined, you can choose your preferred crustacean from the fish tank and your preferred liquid vintage from the visible and impressive wine cellar. As the Cap Horn can be reached by road, it is also open for evening dining. Non-skiers can join in the lunch-time gluttony, as the restaurant will collect you by snowcat.

Those who think **le chalet des pierres** (t 0479 081861) belongs to a group of Peters will realise the real translation when they see it. Situated on the edge of the green (Verdons) piste the "chalet of stones" has a large terrace, facing the majestic Saulire peak - and for less sunny days there is a covered and heated balcony. The highlight for many is the "buffet de patisseries" which has on average 30 delicious puds to choose from each day - and as the lunch service lasts until 4pm you can take your time to enjoy it. With an average spend per head of €50, it is one of the most expensive lunch spots on the mountain. Those with smaller wallets should look underneath the main restaurant to the small **le plage** snack-stop - a stone's throw away but a world apart.

At the top of the Saulire cable car **le panoramic** (t 0479 080088) at 2723m is the valley's highest restaurant and has something to suit all tastes. There is a small kiosk selling drinks and snacks for those allergic to wasting precious skiing time. For the less impatient, there is a self-service restaurant (with indoor and outdoor seating) and a table service restaurant on the upper level for those who believe a skiing holiday is as much about it being a holiday as it is about being able to ski.

Taking its name from an aircraft popular for flying in the Alps, **le pilatus** (t 0479 082049) shares a similar aspect to the Cap Horn, with a view over Grand Blanc - though the food and ambience in this recently renovated mountain chalet is more low-key. A deceptively large restaurant, you can choose to eat on the sunny facing terrace, or indoors in the many rooms or the ugly greenhouse room - its saving grace being the unimpeded view of the arrivals and departures at the nearby altiport.

l'arc en ciel (t 0479 083809) at the top of the Verdons gondola is a basic self-service with a hatch for take-away snacks. Opening hours can be unpredictable.

la bergerie (t 0479 082470) on the edge of the Bellecôte piste has a wonderful slope-side terrace. By day, you can enjoy the delicious food (such as grilled wild salmon) on the sun-warmed terrace and then slump on the inviting sun loungers, before ambling the short distance down the piste to the resort. La Bergerie is also a popular destination for night-time dining. Though originally used to house sheep - hence the name - you can be assured that the interior is now altogether more salubrious. Friday evenings have a Russian theme - with copious amounts of caviar and vodka on the menu to the accompaniment of a "Russian orchestra".

For those who want to DIY there is a **picnic** room at the bottom of the Saulire cable car. On a sunny day, there are fewer better places to sit than at the top of the Creux Noir chairlift. With a plateau at the top, it is the perfect place to enjoy the 360° view, while munching on a baguette.

getting home

All pistes lead to 1850, as do the gondolas, so getting home **on skis** or **by lift** is easy - and you just keep going through 1850 to get to 1550 and Le Praz. To get to 1650 you need to catch one of the Chanrossa, Roc Mugnier or Prameruel chairlifts.

57

courchevel 1650

The eastern side of the Courchevel valley is home to a good selection of pistes and a less pretentious resort life. The runs above the resort are beginner friendly (a collection of greens and blues) and are ideal for novices. Further up the hill there are plenty of fun reds to keep intermediates entertained.

access

Those staying in 1650 need do little more than step on the Ariondaz gondola. The easiest way there from 1550 and Le Praz is to hop on the bus - on skis is a slightly more circuitous route. From 1850 the bus is also an option, or you can ski over to the Roc Mugnier, Prameruel or the Chanrossa chairlifts.

pistes

The only **green** runs are immediately above the resort, and are the perfect learning ground for beginners. For anybody else they are useful only to get to the Ariondaz gondola and go back up again.

blue runs abound in the higher environs, including the 3-line Pyramide, Mont Russe and Plan Mugnier runs, which are rolling hills, suitable for speedsters who want to get some air without too steep a landing. It's hard not to add your own zoom, zoom sound effects as you cruise these motorways.

The **reds** (Chapelets, Rochers and Bel Air) at the easternmost edge of the

map a

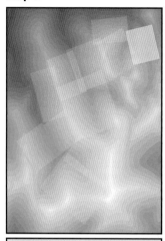

58

---

snapshot

out of interest
highest point - 2700m
aspect - e, n, w
pistes - greens lower down, speedy blues, fantastic reds & 1 black
off-piste - moguls under the chanrossa chair, vallée des avals
restaurants - 2

highlights & hotspots
the bel air restaurant
the chapelets and rochers reds
chairlift access only from the rest of the valley
often quiet pistes
chez le gaulois for lunch

Courchevel valley are probably the best in the whole area. All are long enjoyable descents and are often over-looked - so those who bother can have them to themselves. After a snowfall, you may find these pistes have not been groomed, offering a layer of untracked powder with a firm base underneath. The red (Combe Roc Mugnier) on the other side of the area tends to be busier, and consequently has poorer conditions overall, though its passage through the trees is pretty.

The only **black** is the Chanrossa - from the top of the chairlift of the same name. Conditions can be variable - through ice, moguls and slush.

off-piste

The area under the Chanrossa chair is popular - not least because it is easily accessed. Often mogulled, the snow conditions rarely find an equilibrium between icy and cruddy in the morning and slushy and over-skied by the afternoon - but it is an enjoyable spectacle for the audience on the Chanrossa chair. Further afield, and for the more advanced, the Vallée des Avals offers a number of descents the start of which are reached at the top of the Chanrossa chairlift - none of them should be attempted without a guide.

eating & drinking

The best place for a cheap and quick lunch is in the village itself - **chez le gaulois** serves impossibly delicious

baguettes stuffed with local ham (jambon cru) and hot raclette cheese.

On the piste, **le bel air** (t 0479 080093) at the top of the Ariondaz gondola is a large, sunny chalet, which makes the most of its aspect with a 3-tiered terrace. The food is consistently good and despite the chalet's reasonable size, reservations are generally a good idea.

Offering similar fare to Le Bel Air, **la casserole** (t 0479 080635) has always lost out to its nearest rival because of its appearance. Plans are afoot to transfer the presently ugly, low-lying building into a more aesthetically pleasing wooden chalet with a terrace, to make the most of what sun gets to its position on the edge of the forest, and to tempt customers in to enjoy cuisine that is just as good.

For an indoor **picnic** head to the *salle hors sac* by the lift pass office at the bottom of the 3 Vallées chair.

getting home

Those staying in 1550 and Le Praz can most easily return home by bus. The same is true for 1850 though skiing home is also an option - on the Aiguille de Fruit, Gravelles or Marmottes chairlifts.

59

la tania, le praz & 1550

The west flank of the Courchevel valley is often overlooked - the majority of skiers head up to the Saulire peak or east to 1650. But it has plenty to offer - there are enough runs at the easy level for competent beginners and at the other end of the scale experts will delight in the Jean Blanc and Jockeys blacks. And it is an area of contrast - the view from the top of the Col de la Loze down the Méribel valley has a stunning backdrop of peaks, while lower down the tree-lined slopes are Alpine forests at their best.

access
From the Croisette in 1850 the Chenus gondola takes to the top of the upper pistes in this area. You can also get from 1850 to Le Praz on skis, following the piste through the forest past the bottom of the Plantrey chair. If you want to get to this area quickly from 1650 the bus is generally more speedy than skis - either take it up the hill to the Croisette in 1850 or down the hill to Le Praz.

pistes
In addition to a short stretch in each of 1550, Le Praz and La Tania, there is a series of **green** runs from the top of the Chenus gondola so beginners are not constrained to staying in the lower environs of the area.

The **blue** (Les Folyères) run down through the dense forest to La Tania is the kind of run that can make you feel

map c

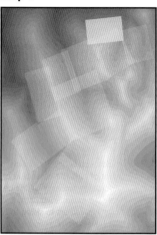

snapshot

out of interest
highest point - 2274 m
aspect - e, n, w
pistes - speedy blues, steep reds & the best blacks in the valley
off-piste - moguls under the dou des lanches chair
restaurants - 4

highlights & hotspots
the old racing runs of jockeys and jean blanc
lower slopes are often bare and unskiable
pretty tree-lined runs
steep draglifts tricky for boarders

crossing the main road to Le Praz's lift station. For most of the season, you should expect the bottom of both to be bare in patches often with branches poking through the snow, but after a heavy snowfall experts don't need to look much further.

off-piste

In this area there is plenty of opportunity to pop off the side of the pistes and dip your booted toe into the powder. The trees in the forests between the Forêt gondola and La Tania gondola have enough space between them to execute some tidy turns - though if there is one time you should wear a helmet it is when you are tree-skiing. For lengthier descents, there are a number of lines to the right of the Dou des Lanches chair - these are popular among the locals and seasonnaires and so get tracked out quickly.

61

like a champion - straight and speedy, it's a whole lot of fun. The other blue of note (Boulevard des Arolles) couldn't be more different - a meandering path, it at least allows newcomers to skiing to feel like they have covered some ground. And they're unlikely to be disturbed.

The **reds** are not as plentiful as those at the top of 1850, but they are often quieter. The Dou des Lanches and Lanches runs generally have better conditions than those lower down the mountain.

The 2 **blacks** (Jockeys and Jean Blanc) are both long and testing and a lot of fun when the snow is good. Both runs finish in Le Praz. The Jockeys run joins the red (Murettes) piste to end by Le Praz's lift station. The Jean Blanc surprisingly ends in the middle of a field - you have to navigate a few back gardens to get to the village, before

eating & drinking

Aside from what's on the mountain, the horseshoe of La Tania offers a number of options, such as the Pub Le Ski Lodge (➔ La Tania). The choices are less obvious in Le Praz, not least because the lift station (and the end of all runs except the Jean Blanc) are some way from the eateries.

The mountain restaurants manage to be cheaper than those within closer range of 1850. **le bouc blanc** (t 0479 088026) is a traditional and homely restaurant at the top of the La Tania gondola and with a large terrace for sunny days. Open 11:30am-4pm it is best to book.

les chenus (t 0479 080684) is one of the few self-service options on this side of the Saulire ridgeline - and it manages to rise above the general expectations. At the top of the Chenus gondola (which starts from 1850's Croisette), it can also be reached by skiing along the blue from the top of the Loze chair. The food available (9am-5pm) is good regional cuisine.

Opened in 1995 **le roc tania** (t 0479 083234, i restaurants-3vallees.com), a chalet-style restaurant does a good job of looking more authentic than its young age suggests. Positioned on the flat Col de la Loze plateau between Méribel and Courchevel it has a fantastic south-west facing terrace, which gets the last rays of the day. The views are fantastic - of the mountains and the parapenters launching from up here. Open 9am-5pm, it is also a good place to stop for après to catch the last rays of the day and watch the sun sink behind the Belleville ridgeline before skiing back to resort.

la soucoupe (t 0479 082134) occupies the site of the first altitude restaurant (Relais de la Loze) in the Courchevel valley. Self-service is available - a bar and pastries for morning, and lunch

from 12pm - but the restaurant on the first floor is the reason to go, and bookings are a good idea. Delightfully rustic if you opt for a steak you can watch it being grilled on the open fire or you can choose from another well-cooked local dish such as diots polenta.

getting home

Home to La Tania is along a blue or a red (or by lift in La Tania gondola from just by the Bouc Blanc restaurant) and to Le Praz the way is red or black (or Le Praz gondola). The most direct to 1550 as the ski glides is the Dou du Midi red from the top of the Plantrey - though you can go via 1850 (on greens or blues) to hop on the Grangettes chairlift or potter home on a blue. If you are short on time and worried about missing the lift connection back to 1650, the bus is always an option.

62

map d

The jagged teeth of the Saulire peaks give the eastern side of the Méribel valley an impressive skyline. At 2738m it is higher than the opposite (Tougnète) side and from the top the eye is treated to a sea of peaks in the Belleville valley and far, far beyond. If you want to spend the afternoon skiing in the sun, head over to this side of the valley - as the slopes face west, the final rays of the day fall here, also making it the better side for sun-baked après, as long as you have organised some transport home. From the top of Saulire there are any number of vertical choices - reds running in parallel to blues interspersed with a few friendly greens and the occasional less friendly black - and the upper slopes are rarely overcrowded. It's difficult to pick a favourite or the best - they all go the same way and on a similar gradient, but if it makes you happy to be on a blue, then there are plenty to choose from. And if you're looking for vertical descents you will find them here - over 1000m from the top of Saulire to Mottaret and another 300m on top of that from the top to La Chaudanne in the centre of Méribel.

access

When it's all systems go with the lift system it is easy to reach the Saulire peak - from 1850 take the Verdons gondola from the Croisette and then the Vizelle gondola or the Saulire cable car, which is also the easiest route from 1550 after an initial trip on the

snapshot

out of interest
highest point - 2738m
aspect - w
pistes - beginner-friendly greens, wide and gentle blues, long and fun red & noir blacks
off-piste - the valley's steepest couloir
restaurants - 7

highlights & hotspots
tree-hugging at the altiport
1300m of vertical descent
après at le rond-point
sunny afternoons
use of your 3 vallées ski pass

Grangettes gondola. From La Tania and Le Praz you can take the same route or hop over to the slopes immediately above Méribel over the ridge at the Col de la Loze - reached by the Dou des Lanches chairlift. From 1650 you can either bus it to 1850 and follow the gondola - gondola/cable car route or go via the top of the Chanrossa chair and then the Marmottes chair.

pistes

64

The best of the valley's **green** pistes are found just above the Altiport. Wide and prettily lined with trees they are very friendly to newcomers to skiing - and they are easily accessed by all along the **blue** from the Col de la Loze. This run can only be described as boring - a long flat path, it is nothing more than the way to get to the skiing lower down from that point on the ridge. The rest of the blues are much more fun - confidence boosting for beginners and speedy for everybody else.

The long **red** (Pic Noir) at the northern end of the valley is one of the most fun runs in the 3 Vallées. Though it is not always open at the beginning of the season (because of inadequate snow coverage), when it is it's a fabulous sweeping descent through the forest to the pistes above the Altiport. At the end you need some speed to avoid an anti-climatic pole. The longest red (Manduit) runs from the top of Saulire to La Chaudanne, the full length of the

mountain, though the very top can be a bit hairy - the steeper gradient turns skiers into mogul creators, not helped by a large rock in the middle of the piste. If you can't avoid the other skiers, you should definitely avoid this at the very least.

There are 3 **black** runs, all of which deserve their grading because of their unpredictable conditions. Tetras from the Col de la Loze is often mogulled and patchy. The Grande Rosière, at the other end of the valley, doesn't get the sun until the afternoon, and often resembles a skating rink for most of the day, as does the Sanglier.

off-piste

Though there are no **itinerary routes** on the official piste map, one that is well known runs through Méribel Village to Brides-les-Bains. Passing through fields and forests, and involving a lot of tree dodging, it is only open if there has been exceptional snowfall - and is only worth the effort so you can say you've done it. Otherwise the Saulire peak offers one of the most serious **off-piste** descents in the valley - the narrow and rocky couloir visible from the Burgin gondola as you ascend to the top. Even steeper than its Courchevel cousins, as it is south facing it is also prone to less favourable conditions especially by the afternoon when the sun has done its damage. Those with more sense than skill will find plenty of ungroomed snow in between the pistes for a taster of the fluffy stuff and some fun can be had tree-dodging through the forest at the Altiport.

eating & drinking

Eating on the mountain isn't one of the highlights of the Méribel valley - the options are pretty samey and pretty pricey for what you get. Eating in the resort is always an option - there are numerous places near La Chaudanne, good hotel restaurants at Le Rond-Point and the Altiport as well as Le Lodge du Village in Méribel Village. In Mottaret, the area around the resort's main hub of lifts turns into a mass picnic site, as many of the slope-side eateries are take-away. Of them the best is the serving hatch at the side of Mottaret's small supermarket, where you can get chicken and chips and hot sandwiches.

le rond-point (t 0479 003751) is a one-stop shop for morning coffee, lunch, and après (if you have organised

some alternative transport home). Ideal for mixed ability groups - it can reached by green, blue or red pistes. Ably run by a predominantly English team, the menu is "international", offering something different from the usual regional specialities - such as wok-fried beef. In clement weather lunch is served on a large terrace. When it is bad, everything moves inside and also upstairs to a charming wooden room under the eaves. For a quick lunch, the snack bar (the Petit Rond-Point) below the main restaurant serves sandwiches and other snacks at reasonable prices (and you can check your emails). Reservations for the à la carte restaurant are essential.

The **adray télébar** hotel (t 0479 086026) on the edge of the Doron piste just below Le Rond-Point is a pleasant spot for lunch, with a lovely south-facing terrace.

At the top of the Altiport button lift, **les rhododendrons** (t 0479 005092) is a large 2 level restaurant with self- and table-service options. With its location at the top of Méribel's nursery slope area, the self-service is often over-crowded with families battling for spaghetti bolognaise before the afternoon lessons begin.

le chardonnet (t 0479 004481) is lovely inside and out and with its wooden beams and stone walls is top of

65

the class for adhering strictly to Méribel's architectural rules. The food is pleasant but suffers from typically French and very slow service.

Slightly lower down the hill is **le choucas** (t 0479 005831). Built in 1962 this was the first mountain restaurant in the valley. Situated at the Burgin gondola mid-station, if you're looking for a late breakfast, try the "oeufs choucas".

66

At the top of the Pas du Lac 2 gondola, **les pierres plates** (t 0479 004641) is the highest restaurant on Saulire and the best thing about it is the view over to Mont du Vallon and beyond. Because of its location it is a great place to catch the last of the sunshine before an alcohol injected ski home, but beware the strength of the *rhum chocolat*.

côte 2000 (t 0479 005540) is the last slope-side stop on the descent down from Saulire to Mottaret - though if you are not taken by the menu you need only ski a little further to the resort and the numerous choices there.

If you object to spending £20 for a croque-monsieur and a coke, a **picnic** is an alternative. And as there are benches at the top of the Col de la Loze plateau, by the Burgin gondola mid-station and at various points in the forest around the Altiport it is a fairly civilised option.

For après the **rond-point** with its live music is the obvious choice and the only place on this side of the mountain where you find live bands. A more civilised alternative is just up the hill - in the **yéti** hotel, with its delightful terrace overlooking the pistes. If you decide to have a drink after the lifts close you can get a bus back to the Courchevel valley in the early evening - though if you miss it you will need to hail a cab.

getting home

For those staying in 1850 and 1550 once you get to the top of Saulire (using either the Burgin gondola or the Pas du Lac gondola from Mottaret), all you have to do is point your skis down the hill to home. If you're staying in 1650 don't forget that you have to catch an additional lift (any of the Chanrossa, Roc Mugnier or Prameruel chairlifts) before you are into the skiing above the resort. The quickest way to get home to La Tania and Le Praz is via the Col de la Loze - take the Loze chairlift to get there - from where you ski home or continue your journey by lift on the Dou des Lanches chairlift.

If your legs don't fancy the ski home, you can get back to 1850 or 1550 by lift - the Saulire cable car and then the Verdons gondola (followed by the Grangettes gondola to 1550). For the rest your legs will just have to keep going.

Méribel's Tougnète side wakes up in the sun (on good weather days) so if you like to avoid the morning ice, this is one place to head. The ridge is the divide between Méribel and the Belleville valley and the skiing above the resorts of Les Menuires and St. Martin de Belleville.

access

The main lifts up to the skiing on Tougnète begin at La Chaudanne in Méribel - so that is where you should head from any of the Courchevel resorts. Once there, there are 3 ways to get up the mountain - so take your pick depending upon weather and queues. The most direct route to the very top is by the Tougnète gondola, which ends at the top of the ridge - and the top of a blue, red or black run, so there is something for everybody.

pistes

The only **green** is the Truite, which links Méribel to Mottaret - and is often festooned with beginners.

There are loads of **blues** - though all are much of a muchness in terms of gradient and nature.

The **reds** are fewer but fun - all follow a similar line down the mountain from the top of the Tougnète ridge.

One of the enduring remains of the 1992 Winter Olympics is the Face **black** run. Conditions are variable - not only daily but at different points on the run

map e

67

snapshot

out of interest
highest point - 2434m
aspect - e
pistes - a very flat green, plentiful blues, plentiful reds & the resort's most famous black
off-piste - itinerary route to les allues
restaurants - 3

highlights & hotspots
the olympic (face) black
the moonpark
can be cold in the afternoon in early winter
easily accessed off-piste

itself. The black called Les Bosses ('bosses' is French for moguls) lives up to its name. Higher up, Combe Tougnète starts off steep, though it looks worse from the approach lift (the Tougnète 2 gondola) than it actually is.

snowpark

One of the 2 snowparks in the valley, and regarded as the best, at the Moonpark de L'Arpasson you will find 2 half-pipes (1 competition standard and 1 for those not quite so good), a number of graded jumps and a 1km boardercross. It's less busy than the snowpark above Mottaret (➥ Mont du Vallon) so it's the perfect place to try out your tricks in (relative) private.

68

off-piste

An **itinerary route** runs from the top of Roc de Fer down to Le Raffort and ultimately the village of Les Allues. It is only skiable after a lengthy dump of snow, but is neither particularly difficult nor easy.

eating & drinking

As for the Saulire side of the mountain you can ski down to the centre of Méribel for lunch. One option is **les castors** (t 0479 085279) a long-standing and local-run restaurant at the foot of the green (Truite) piste. Sit down meals and take-away are possible.

les crêtes (t 0479 085650/0609 405104) is a low-slung, cosy little

restaurant on the top of the Tougnète ridge. Cuisine is traditional and the restaurant is known for its Tartiflette (a potato-based dish) - one of the best ways to warm up the extremities. On sunny days the views from the terrace are awesome - although as the restaurant terrace has a fairly exposed aspect it is rarely enjoyable.

arpasson (t 0479 004348) near stage 1 of the Tougnète gondola offers both table and self-service. The terrace is pleasant for an afternoon vin chaud as you return down the mountain.

For official **picnics** take your sandwiches to the benches at the top of the Caves lift. For something more spontaneous just pick a patch of snow.

getting home

As for 'access', getting home involves a trip via La Chaudanne. For those staying in 1850 and 1550 the Burgin gondola takes you to the top of Saulire and the top of your descent home - it's the same for those staying on 1650, with a trip on the Chanrossa, Roc Mugnier or Prameruel chairlifts. Those staying in La Tania and Le Praz can also go via Saulire - and once down in the Courchevel valley, take the Coqs chairlift - or over the Col de la Loze (take the Rhodos gondola and then the Loze chairlift).

If you had to describe the skiing on Mont du Vallon in 1 word it would be 'long'. Lovely, lengthy lines unfold from the peak - though this guide uses the name to describe the skiing in the surrounding area as well. From Mont du Vallon to the bottom of the Mûres Rouges chairlift is around 1100m and from the top of the Plattières gondola it is 1000m to Mottaret. The north facing aspect keeps the snow light and powdery but because of the altitude (2952m at the top), the area is sensitive to inclement weather - if bad weather hits, it hits here first. Mont du Vallon closes at the first rumour of a breeze, as does the Côte Brune chairlift, and with it any chance of getting to Val Thorens. One side of the Mont du Vallon peak is home to the beautiful Reserve Naturelle de Tueda, a national park in which no skiing is permitted - if you do venture in and are caught you can be heavily fined. The only drawback to the area is that the runs are used by skiers staying in the Courchevel and Méribel valleys to get to the skiing around the resort of Val Thorens - and then at the end of the day to get home so they can be very busy.

access

The easiest way to reach the Mont du Vallon peak is by taking the Plattières gondola out of Mottaret to its second stage. Whichever Courchevel resort you are coming from, the most direct way is via the Saulire peak - as the runs down to Mottaret start from there.

map f

69

snapshot

out of interest
highest point - 2952m
aspect - n, e
pistes - a range of very flat to fairly steep blues, lengthy reds & a lone black
off-piste - numerous itinerary routes & shortcuts between pistes
restaurants - 3

highlights & hotspots
lovely, long descents
bottlenecks at the plan des mains chairlift
vulnerable to bad weather
light and powdery snow

mont du vallon

pistes

green is not a colour that appears on this part of the piste map and so **blue** is as easy as it gets and the range in difficulty is extensive. Both boarders and skiers should beware the frustratingly flat track (Ours) - though this has been improved for the 2004 season - through the forest from the bottom of the Mûres Rouges chairlift to Mottaret. Its pancake tendancies have been the flatfall (rather than downfall) of many a man.

red alert - they are numerous in this area. The highlight is the duo from the top of the Mont du Vallon peak. The 5kms Combe du Vallon run is the longer of the two - but be aware you need to take the Mûres Rouges chairlift back up or face the blue Ours run - but neither suffers for lack of vertical descent.

The Bartavelle is the sole **black** - a relatively short descent and pales in comparison with the reds.

snowpark

A bigger snowpark than the Moonpark above Méribel, it is more suited to those having a go for the first time. The flipside of this is that it is often busier. It has a better defined 4-man boardercross - complete with a starting platform - making it more of a fun-park in some ways. With 2 half-pipes and 2 quarter pipes, it has excellent terrain for getting air. One word of advice - be confident of your tricks as the park is

laid out underneath the Plattières gondola so you have an airbourne audience willing you to take a fall.

off-piste

Mont du Vallon is home to a number of **itinerary routes** - though none are marked on the resort's official piste map. Conditions on them are generally regarded as better later on in the season - when there can be glorious spring snow. There are also plenty of off-piste shortcuts between the 2 red runs down from the peak, which make for enjoyable practise, as well as the same underneath the third stage of the Plattières gondola, the Côte Brune chairlift and the Plan des Mains chair. If you decide to venture off-piste take notice of the avalanche warnings.

eating & drinking

la sitelle (t 0479 004348) is the slope-side equivalent of a motorway service station - used mainly for pit and loo

70

stops. On the left side of the main blue run down into Mottaret, its large terrace is too far into the shadow of the mountain to get any afternoon sun.

Both self- and table service are on offer in **le mont de la chambre** (t 0479 006768), a higgledy-piggledy place at the top of the Côte Brune chair and the junction to Val Thorens. And after a ride on the aforementioned and cruelly exposed lift you may well need to worship at the temple of the goddess of hot chocolate - available from the bar just inside the entrance. Food from both sections is consistently good value.

le roc des 3 marches (t 0479 004648) is a standard self-service at the top of the Plattières gondola. Though it has a terrace, thanks to its exposed position you are unlikely to use it.

le chalet de togniat (t 0479 004511) at the bottom of the Roc de Tougne draglifts is a good and generally quiet restaurant with a pleasant terrace.

This area is a haven for tupperware lovers, with **picnic** spots galore - surprising given that it suffers most from bad, bad weather. There are 4 official sites to unwrap your ham butties - at the bottom of the Mont du Vallon gondola, at the top of the second stage of the Plattières gondola, at the top of the Côte Brune chairlift and at the top of the Roc de Tougne 1 & 2 button lifts.

getting home

The Plan des Mains chair is the link between the pistes on and around the Mont du Vallon peak - if you are too late to catch this lift the flat Ours run is a tiring alternative. From the top of the chair the home run to Mottaret is blue. And once in Mottaret you can catch the Pas du Lac gondola to the top of Saulire. If you plan to return by lift you can hop onto the Plattières gondola at the top of the Plan des Mains chairlift - it ends in Mottaret where you can switch onto the Pas du Lac.

71

If the 3 Vallées were the setting for a fairytale, St. Martin de Belleville would be Cinderella and Val Thorens and Les Menuires the ugly sisters. An old and charming village, and the lowest resort in the Belleville valley, there is the sense of it having been home to a community long before the hordes of winter pleasure seekers descended. From the top of the Tougnète ridge the view is of a series of gently rolling ski fields - the snow disguises what is actually grazing pasture and as you descend the mountain you pass ramshackled farmers' huts.

72

access
From any of the resorts in the Courchevel valley, the easiest way to get to St. Martin is through Méribel's La Chaudanne - take the Tougnète gondola to the top of the ridge with the Belleville valley.

pistes
The pistes are few in number and scary is not a word that would be used to describe them - but their length make up for their scarcity and the scenery more than compensates for their moderation. **green** is not a colour that appears on the piste map, though there are enough **blues** to keep beginners or nervous intermediates happy. The long Liaison/Gros Tougne is best avoided by boarders who will become frustrated with the narrowness and level gradient of the path - even skiers may need to pole in places - unless they are

map g

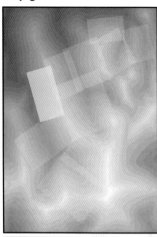

snapshot

out of interest
highest point - 2704m
aspect - w
pistes - no greens, long blues, rolling reds & no blacks
off-piste - gentle sloped snowfields
restaurants - 2

highlights & hotspots
quiet pistes
the charming village of st. martin
the michelin starred la bouitte
the boring liaison and gros tongue blues
the lengthy and exciting jerusaleum red

attempting to get to Les Menuires. All of the **reds** are found up high - the highlight is Jerusaleum, a rarely busy and always enjoyable descent that normally has good conditions.

off-piste

From the top of the Olympic chair the gentle gradient of wide open snow fields makes it ideal for leisurely off-piste skiing - though watch out for sudden drops in the terrain (cliffs!) and don't venture too far beyond the right extent of the area, or you face a long trek back to civilisation.

eating & drinking

The village of St. Martin offers some lovely spots for lunch, most noticeably **le grenier** at the hotel St. Martin - and if you have time, the charming village is worth exploring. But make sure you don't miss your lift home, as it's a costly (time and money) journey home by road. Those seeking something to remind themselves of home should try **brewski's**, known for its pies and chicken curry. For a truly gastronomic Michelin-starred lunch take the off-piste route down to the hamlet of Saint-Marcel and head for the **la bouitte** (t 0479 089677) - the restaurant will send a minibus to pick you up from the roadside at St. Martin if conditions are not good enough to ski to the door.

On the way down the mountain you pass **les crêtes** (➥ tougnète) while further down still, where the top of the

St. Martin 1 gondola meets the bottom of the St. Martin 2 chairlift you will find **le chardon bleu** (t 0479 089536) and **le corbeleys** (t 0479 089531). Both are rustic in appearance - having had former lives as mountain huts - and serve similar ranges of Bellevilloises and Savoyarde specialities. On the last stretch of the blue run down to St. Martin you pass the large-terraced **la loë** (t 0479 089272), which serves cheap omelettes and salads.

getting home

73

As for 'access' it is easiest to return to the Courchevel valley through La Chaudanne in Méribel. To get there take the St. Martin 2 chairlift to the top of Tougnète from where you can ski down or take the lift (the Tougnète gondola) to La Chaudanne.

A modern purpose-built resort, Les Menuires is a interesting mix of architectural designs. Following the mixed reaction to the post-modernist church the architects of the newer buildings have taken some lessons from its prettier neighbours, constructing wooden chalets instead of monolithic tower-block monstrosities - though the damage to the skyline has already been done. A favourite with families, the layout of the ski area has convenience in mind - the lifts run up the hill in a series of vertical lines and the numerous pistes run down in a similar fashion to merge in a tangled mess above the resort centre.

74

access

Though the Belleville valley runs parallel to the Méribel valley, Les Menuires is more in-line with Mottaret than Méribel - though you can reach it from both resorts. From Méribel the top of the Tougnète gondola brings you out at the top of the most direct route to Les Menuires - the aptly named Gros Tougne, a long and boring blue which is flat in places. From Mottaret take either the Plattières gondola to the top of the Roc des 3 Marches or the Côte Brune chairlift to the top of Mont de la Chambre - from the top of both you can ski down to Les Menuires. Those who don't feel confident enough to ski the top runs, can always descend towards Les Menuires in the Bruyères gondola - easier blue pistes are accessible from its mid-station.

map h

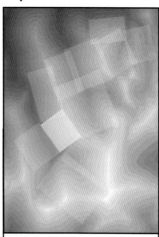

snapshot

out of interest
highest point - 2850m
aspect - w
pistes - mini greens, safe-as-houses blues, numerous and lengthy reds & surprisingly tricky blacks
off-piste - limited
restaurants - 6

highlights & hotspots
the views
the long and boring access piste from méribel
the covered mont de la chambre chair
chaotic slopes during school holidays

pistes

The few **greens** are at resort level, as are the majoirty of the **blues**. The quietest is generally the Mont de la Chambre at the far end of the area - it also generally has the best conditions, as the others closer to the resort suffer from over-use. The blues below the resort are worth disregarding altogether as they are little more than access pistes to the skiing on La Masse (the ski slopes on the opposite side of the valley from Les Menuires) or the small areas of accommodation below the main resort.

Of the **reds** Les 4 Vents can live up to its name, while the rest are simliar in nature - long and generally enjoyable descents that are on the top edge of the red bracket.

The **blacks** too are surprisingly tricky given the family-tastic nature of the resort. All can be icy but they are seldom busy.

off-piste

As so much of this area is groomed even the piste-side off-piste is limited. If that is what you are looking for you should head down the valley to St. Martin or back over the ridge to Méribel.

eating & drinking

There are plenty of pit-stops in the resort itself, most of which are ideally placed on the side of the piste, so you don't have to venture too far from the snow. One of them is the English-run **sphère** bar and restaurant, which serves food 12pm-3:30pm - you can also check your emails at their internet station if you don't like being out of touch for too long.

les quatre vents (t 0479 006444) on the hill is decorated throughout with stuffed animals eerily preserved as if mid-movement - which can be a little disconcerting as you tuck into your frites - though the the advert outside suggests this menagerie is something the restaurant is proud of. Once you get accustomed to their glassy stares the reasonably good self-service food (and good made-to-order omelettes) is reasonably priced and the staff are friendly.

The **chalet du capricorne** (t 0479 006510) just below Les Menuires provides architectural relief from the rest of the resort - a small slope-side cabin on the blue piste down towards La Masse/Le Bettex - the menu is similar to what you find elsewhere.

getting home

As for 'access' it is easier to get home through Mottaret. The Mont de la Chambre chair and the Bruyères gondola both end at the top of Mont de la Chambre and the top of the main descent to Mottaret. Returning home by lift is not an option from here. To do that you need to pass over the ridge at the Roc des 3 Marches.

75

la masse

La Masse is opposite Les Menuires and is the chalk to its cheese. The masses generally don't bother so there are no family-littered pistes here, just a handful of reds and blacks that are generally quiet and in generally excellent condition. One of the best destinations for intermediate and expert skiers, La Masse, being east facing, is best for morning skiing as it falls into shadow by the afternoon - though as it is some distance from Courchevel you will be lucky to get there before midday. There are many short stretches of off-piste in between the slopes for those looking for powder. The view from the top of the highest peak is also one of the best - an expanse of further peaks and snow fields and the beginning of some of the area's most enjoyable itinerary routes. Even if you don't fancy skiing the steepish reds and blacks from the top it is worth going up for the view.

access

As La Masse lies on the far side of the Belleville valley, you first pass through the Méribel valley. As for Les Menuires the quickest way to get there is through Mottaret. Once in Les Menuires look for a gap in the semi-circle of commerce at the bottom of the pistes - the piste through this gap leads down to the lift links to La Masse.

pistes

That there are no **green** pistes sums up the spirit of La Masse. The only **blue** of

76

map i

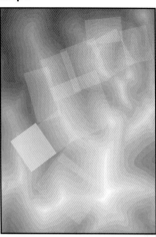

significance is the Vallons run from the top of the Rocher Noir chairlift - and it is generally the busiest piste in the area. For **reds** you are spoilt for choice and can descend from top to bottom by red alone - up high the Fred Covill run from the top of the Masse 2 gondola, and then Les Enverses to the bottom of the Rocher Noir chair.

Of the 2 **blacks** found here the Dame Blanche has the most to offer - a steepish descent on the far right side of the area it is accessed on the Masse draglift, which is not always open. The Lac Noir from the top of the chair of the same name is probably only graded black because it is narrow.

off-piste

The off-piste accessible from the top of La Masse has the reputation of being some of the best in the area. The choice of routes is varied so you can make it as hard as you want it to be, and it is one way to get away from the manufactured feel of Les Menuires. A number of routes pass through the Vallée of Entremont which is still home to farming communities and herds of cattle - and which you may ski past (or through) during the spring months. Also from the back of La Pointe de la Masse (the area's highest point) you can reach St. Martin de Belleville by heading down the Col de Fenêtre.

eating & drinking

There are 3 options for food and drink -

le panoramic (t 0479 228060) at the very top, **les roches blanches** (t 0479 006022) mid-way down and **les 3V** (t 0479 007404) towards the bottom. Le Panoramic is a cosy little place where you are likely to come across groups of ski adventurers about to descend into the endless off-piste down the backside of the peak. Les Roches Blanches is more of a haunt for intermediate skiers. A pleasant self-service, it has a large terrace outside from where you can admire what you have just come down. Inside there is a sweet mezzanine level where you can warm up with a plate of frites and a coke. Les 3V is also self-service, and one which upsets the stereotype. The food served is excellent - a range of hearty soups, decent slabs of French cheese and home-made puddings, all of which can be eaten on the lovely terrace on the edge of the piste.

77

getting home

As for Les Menuires the easiest way home is through Mottaret. At the bottom of La Masse take the Doron chair or the Croisette gondola to get back to the lifts from Les Menuires that will take you home. You can't get from the very top of La Masse to the bottom by lift - unless you fancy walking from the bottom of La Masse 2 gondola to the top of La Masse 1 gondola.

The highest resort in not only the 3 Vallées but also the European Alps, and (logically) the highest skiing in the 3 Vallées - 3200m at the top of the Cime de Caron. It is the only valley in which the pistes are on a glacier. Situated at the top end of the Belleville valley, and surrounded by a half-moon crescent of mountains, the skiing is wide and open. Its altitude makes it susceptible to changeable weather - it is not unusual to bask in sunshine in Méribel and find Val Thorens shrouded in cloud - so dress warm. Val Thorens is not for the aesthete: the area is desolate without a tree in sight - and compared to the picture postcard charm of Méribel the resort is something of a monstrosity.

78

In recent years the valley over the ridge from Cime de Caron has been tamed. A great destination for those suffering from cabin fever, claustrophobia or just looking to escape from the masses - it is the only valley where you can enjoy the feeling of quiet isolation without the extra challenge of being off-piste. On a clear day the views are stunning with very little urbanisation in sight. During a good season, you can ski down to the small village of Orelle.

access

The skiing above Val Thorens is the least easy to reach. The resorts of Courchevel and Méribel lie vaguely parallel to each other within their valley so linkage between them is easy. Val

map j & k

snapshot

out of interest
highest point - 3230m
aspect - all
pistes - resort-level greens, long blues, longer reds & steep or bumpy blacks
off-piste - extensive: couloirs, glaciers & bowls
restaurants - 12

highlights & hotspots
the cime de caron black
the 4th valley
susceptible to windy conditions
consequently often closed

Thorens by contrast is actually some way further away. From Courchevel the most direct route is through Mottaret and the Mont du Vallon area. Take the Plattières gondola to its second stage, ski down the Bouvreil run (blue or red depending upon your ability) to the bottom of the Côte Brune chairlift. This brings you out at the top of Mont de la Chambre, and the crossroads of runs back down to Mottaret and to Val Thorens. Boarders will need to get up some speed on the flat approach run from the top towards Val Thorens.

To reach Maurienne, ski through the Val Thorens resort and take the Moutière chair and then the Funitel Grand Fond - the entrance to the 4th valley is through a stone-blasted opening in the rock, which may well remind you of Harry Potter. Alternatively you can take the Caron gondola followed by the Cime de Caron cable car, though this way you are committed to skiing a black run.

pistes

The pistes immediately around Val Thorens are all **green**, which makes reaching the rest of the area child's play.

The approach runs from the Méribel valley are mainly **blue** - and all are long and fun. Those around the resort are similar, though some are flat enough to justify a green grade. The 2 blues in the 4th valley are generally enjoyable too - though the Gentianes down into the valley is track-like in places.

The valley is home to oodles of **reds**. Those on the Pèclet glacier are very popular - generally have the best conditions and such even terrain that you can reach some fairly high speeds. The reds from the Breche de Rosaël are ideal for carving practise as are those from the Boismint and Plan de l'Eau chairs, which are generally the quietest in the area.

Val Thorens is home to probably the best **black** in the 3 Vallées ski area, the long and speedy Cime de Caron. Starting at 3200m, this sweeps down under the shadow of the peak of the same name. Being reasonably sheltered and north-facing, the conditions are generally good, though susceptible to some icy patches. Over in the 4th valley the only black (Combe Rosaël) runs from the top of the Cime de Caron and had a previous existence as an itinerary route.

snowpark

The Val Thorens snowpark is small compared to those in the Méribel valley - and it is not steep enough to get any serious air. The boardercross in the 4th valley is not obviously marked nor always open, but finding your own line down it can be fun.

summer skiing

Val Thorens is one of the few resorts in European that is open during the summer for skiing. The Pèclet glacier sees some snow 365 days a year and

79

though the skiing is limited a summer holiday in Val Thorens is certainly different from the usual trip to the beach.

off-piste
The Val Thorens has plenty of piste-side powder - particularly around the boardercross course in the 4th valley - and it provides the start to a number of excellent off-piste itineraries and glacier skiing. At the bottom end of the valley is the Lac du Lou - the area between Val Thorens and La Masse. If you start at the top of the Cime de Caron the vertical descent is over 1000m - though pick your route at the bottom carefully and you may end up in somewhere very icy and cold. The 4th valley has enough off-piste to keep you going for the whole of your stay - to make sure you see the best of it take a guide.

eating & drinking
le chalet du thorens (t 0479 000280) is a big venture with a mass market feel. Maze-like in layout, there are enough choices to confuse even the least weather-beaten skier. Options include table-service Savoie specialities, self-services standards and take-away paninis from the stall outside.

le galoubet (t 0479 000048), in the heart of the resort, is easy to spot - its huge outdoor terrace is festooned with green umbrellas. Located on the right hand side of the resort as you ski

through it you can grab a take-away sandwich on your way.

le chalet de caron (t 0479 000171) is one of the better self-service restaurants in the 3 Vallées. The choice of food is wide and reasonably priced with a good salad buffet and the usual *saucisson et frites*. There is a huge terrace outside for sunny days and an equally large seating area inside.

l'oxalys (t 0479 001200) next to Club Med's Val operation, on the side of the Cairn piste, has a south-facing terrace and a good reputation. As the chef is something of an experimenter (making interesting use of ingredients) this is not your usual slope-side eating experience - it is not unusual to find liquorice in the same dish as potatoes. And, in an otherwise cheap Val Thorens, the bill reflects the care and attention given.

la moutière (t 0479 000267) is a lovely piste-side cabin at the top of the lift of the same name. Dog lovers will delight in the very friendly resident hound.

On the Cascade piste **le bar de la marine** (t 0479 000312) is a good service restaurant with a nautical theme and an owner with a very well-tended moustache.

If you are skiing at the lower end of the valley **le chalet des 2 ours** (t 0479 011409) on the Boismint piste is more than adequate lunch. At the other extreme of the area **l'altiself 3000** (t 0479 000376) is one of the 2 places in the valley where you can have lunch on a glacier. **l'étape 3200** (t 0607 310414) is the other and takes the accolade of being the highest mountain restaurant in the whole of the 3 Vallées.

Just off the run of the same name **le chalet de genépi** (t 0479 000328) below the Moraine chair-lift has an open fire inside and good views from its sunny terrace.

Over in the 4th valley, the **plan bouchet refuge** (t 0479 568808) is the only lunch-stop and is proof that although the lifts are here the spirit of the rest of the 3 Vallées has yet to follow. A very basic self-service restaurant, it is likely to be filled with gnarly mountain men, rather than fur-clad Parisiennes. That said, the food fills a hole. And there is a microwave, should you have remembered to throw a ready meal into your backpack at the start of the day. It is also possible to stay the night here (and make the most of having made the lengthy trip from Courchevel) if you remembered to throw in a sleeping bag as well.

As you need to make several lifts to get back to Courchevel après around Val Thorens is not advised. And if you're in the 4th valley for après, you're in trouble on 2 counts - the venues are non-existent and you've got a long and expensive journey home. Never has "one for the road" been so literal.

getting home

There are a variety of routes home. You can go through Les Menuires - ski down the Boulevard Cumin, which links the 2 resorts. The more direct way is over the Col de la Chambre - take the Bouquetin lift to the top. Save some energy for the journey home as there is a long ski down the Lac de la Chambre red until you reach you next lift link - the Plan des Main chair. If by then your legs have given out you can catch the Plattières gondola from its second stage back down to Mottaret.

Though you can get into the 4th valley from the top of the Cime de Caron cable car, you can only return by the Rosaël peak - there is no lift link back up to the Cime de Caron. Boarders should expect a bit of a walk from the top of the Rosaël chairlift.

And finally. If you miss the last lift take your wallet - a taxi from Val Thorens to Courchevel costs a purse-shattering €200. The alternative is a slow bus journey to Moûtiers.

81

So many pistes, so little time. Often it's difficult to know where to start, where to find the longest runs, or where to go when there's not much snow or the weather is bad. Here are a few suggestions.

the first morning
There are pistes within easy reach of all of the resorts which are suitable for finding your ski legs, though those staying in 1650 probably have it best. In addition to the full monty of friendly blues and reds the pistes are often quieter than those around 1850 - so fewer people will see you first tentative turns (or tumbles).

3 vallées marathon
This one takes a bit of planning - requiring an early start and attention to lift times on the way home - and is not for the first day of your stay. Where you start depends on where you are staying. If the aim is to touch the far corner of Val Thorens and get home in time for tea, the most direct route from the Courchevel valley is through Mottaret - cross the ridgeline at Saulire. For the delights of La Masse on the far side of Les Menuires you can pop down through Méribel - crossing the ridge at either Saulire of the Col de la Loze - and make your approach from the top of the Tougnète gondola. Wherever you decide to go, the only thing that will spoil a day exploring the full extent of the area is

getting stuck in the wrong valley - your only way back will be by road courtesy of an expensive taxi ride.

bad weather
When the snow falls and the wind blows, everything above the tree line is vulnerable to the onslaught. But that shouldn't leave you feeling glum. Storms are almost a reason to rejoice in the Courchevel valley - the old racing runs of Jean Blanc and Jockeys through the trees to Le Praz can be at their best when the snow is swirling. And thanks to its lower altitude the Le Praz gondola often runs when lifts higher up are having a day off.

take the trail gourmand
Few of the menus in the Courchevel valley are designed with dieters in mind - so it is difficult to choose just one restaurant as the place for epicurean delights. At least this means you can plan your skiing day around

82

your stomach. Over in 1650 the Bel-Air never fails to please while t'other side Le Soucoupe at the top of the Plantrey fare offers hearty but gastro mountain fare in delightful surroundings. For a fix of aphrodisiacs don't miss the seafood platters at Le Cap Horn. And if you've got room and need a good pud to round off your day head to Le Chalet des Pierres and its buffet table of over 30 tarts and desserts - fortunately served until 4pm should it take you some time to get from your lunch venue.

get an award

The resorts and the ESF have designated certain points in the 3 valleys as "must-sees" - 16 in total, listed on a "discovery card" which is available from any office of the ESF. Once your card has 16 ticks - your visits being certified by your (ESF) instructor at the end of each day - you get your very own shiny 3 Vallées

medal. And though to some this may seem like a cynical ploy to get you to book lessons at least you'll have made the most of your 3 Vallées lift pass - and seen some of the most beautiful parts of the area.

hem yourself in

A suggestion for experts only - and then only those with nerves of steel. The couloirs visible from the top of the Saulire ridge have something of a magnetic draw for advanced skiers. Ranging from a black piste to a slope with a 35º pitch these rock-encased corridors are not for the claustrophobic and it's a good idea to practise your short swing turns before you attempt them. Bon chance.

something for the kids

The slopes above 1850 are an ideal place to introduce tiny tots to skiing. The lower pistes are all graded green, all end at the Croisette - so there is little danger of losing your child - and most are serviced by gentle button lifts. Higher up the hill the enclosed slopes of Ferme and Altiport are also somewhere children can learn in safety - and the nearby wigwam will cheer up those who find snowploughs too tricky to master or the cold a little unpalatable. Nippers someway up the ability chain will delight in the "flying carpet" fun park - a series of rolling hills underneath the Verdons gondola. Expect whoops and squeals.

83

off-piste & touring

Despite its fame as a skier's paradise the 3 Vallées is not the first place you'd think of for gnarly off-piste. As so much of the area is groomed the true off-piste takes a little bit of effort to find. Piste-side powder-poachers can take their pick - many runs have open space off to the side. Hikers will not find marked itineraries like in Verbier or Zermatt, but hiring a guide will reveal a world of powder trails both well known and not.

The descriptions below are intended only to whet the appetite...

84

The obvious starting point for off-piste skiing in the Courchevel valley is the line of couloirs from the Saulire ridgeline. Couloir skiing is only for those who are confident that their turns will happen where they need them to. The first 2 couloirs from the top of the cable car station are known as Téléphérique and the Emilie Allais - though maybe warm up first on the third one along, the pisted and somewhat wider Grand Couloir. Further along the ridge are the even steeper Curé couloir and the even less accessible Verdons Cross couloir. If at the bottom that seemed like a walk in the park the couloir on the other side of Saulire (and known as the Elevator Shaft) down towards Méribel should leave you less able to say 'no fear'. As this is south-facing and narrow, it is best avoided after a sunny stretch and particularly heavy snow. Back over in the Courchevel valley, the route (known to the English as 'Plumbers Crack')

above the Col de la Loze is one of the most famous off-piste descents - the hike to get up there can be take you 30 minutes-1 hour, depending upon your own fitness and which couloir takes your fancy. The site of the Courchevel Freeride competition, it is avalanche prone. Towards 1650 the Vallée des Avals in the Vanoise National Park is known not only for its off-piste routes but also for its stunning beauty. As the descents into this valley - accessed from the top of the Chanrossa chairlift take you into a remote wilderness go with a guide. Closer to home, the Creux bowl - reached from the top of the Creux Noirs chairlift - offers some wide and sustained skiing though be aware that avalanches are common and boarders may find themselves with quite a walk out at the bottom.

As with any off-piste skiing, the usual precautions should be taken. For fuller descriptions of these routes see the book 'Les 3 Vallées Hors pistes - Off piste' by Philippe Baud and Benoit Loucel.

Though ski tourers are not as common a sight in Courchevel as in resorts such as Chamonix, there is still plenty to be done - from half day hikes to overnight tours. The Courchevel Bureau des Guides offers a number of hikes and the ESF in 1850 offers an off-piste programme - including an introduction to off-piste and ski touring and a freeride course for the more proficient.

events

The Courchevel valley is only a small speck on the Alpine events calendar - most only attract a local following or are designed to entertain holidaymakers.

One of the most spectacular is the **courchevel freeride championship** - when top-class skiers descend the Rocher de la Loze (the peak above the Col de la Loze plateau). Best enjoyed with a picnic and a camera.

If the timing of your trip coincides with a **ski jump** competition, it is worth a look. The impressive jump in Le Praz was built for the 1992 winter Olympics in Albertville and watching skiers hurtling down it will make you realise Eddie 'the Eagle' Edwards wasn't that bad after all. The question most ask, is how do you know you can do it?

The **3 vallées rally** at the end of the season is a team event for pros, amateurs and children. A series of races (derbies, skiercross, free-ride) is held throughout the area - contact the tourist office for more details.

The Mountain Centre in La Tania holds a **dual slalom challenge** (in association with Natives ➥ seasonnaires) which attracts the more talented seasonnaires and a party atmosphere.

activities

There are a number of companies in the valley dedicated to organising **torchlit descents**, **ice karting** and **snowmobiling** - try Animation Services (t 0479 220107, i animationservices.net) or Chardon Loisirs (t 0479 083960, i chardonloisirs.com). If you fancy a spot of tobogganing and find all sledges have been hijacked by the more organised **bumboarding** is an option - - the snow equivalent of body-surfing, you rely on your own posterior to get you down the slope.

The 3 Vallées has over 100kms of **cross-country** tracks, 66kms of which are in the Courchevel valley, so you have a lot of ground to cover. Those who doubt their technique can book a lesson with the ESF. **snowshoeing** is an alternative way to discover the valley's forests and wildlife. Guided hikes are bookable through the ESF or Raquette Evasion (t 0479 220422/0680 335611, i raquette-evasion.com). Alternatively you can DIY using the map produced by the tourist office showing all of the marked trails (17kms in total). Snowshoes can be hired from the bigger sport stores.

As **heliskiing** is forbidden by law in France, you are better saving your cash until you find yourself in a resort such as Verbier or Zermatt or better still North America. The Bureau des Guides and Ski Prestige (t 0479 221117, i skiprestige.com) will organise heli-skiing trips, though you inevitably spend some time getting to the drop-off point.

the resort

When you're not on the slopes, how hectic your holiday is depends very much on which resort you are staying in. As with most things, Courchevel takes eating out very seriously and the variety of **restaurants** is extensive. In this part of France, traditional Savoyard food (fondue, tartiflette, braserade, pierre chaude and raclette) is almost inescapable. If you are keen to try one of the Savoie recipes make sure you take a friend, as without exception they can only be ordered for a minimum of 2 people. How much you pay for your fondue depends entirely upon what altitude you eat it at - though it tastes the same wherever you are you will pay twice as much for it in 1850 as you will in 1650. Most of the restaurants are French owned. In the lower villages where most people are on a chalet holiday it's a good idea to book a table on 'chalet night off' - typically Wednesday - when the Camillas and Carolines will be putting their culinary skills into vodka sampling. At lunchtime most places have a plat du jour and some offer a fixed-price menu. Many restaurants have terraces which are fine for a morning coffee or lunch only, as by mid-afternoon most have fallen into the shade, putting a chill on your hot chocolate and vin chaud. If you're feeling peckish long before supper time, it's not hard to get your hands in a decent piece of cake (it being France) - the difficult bit is choosing which 1 (or 3) to eat. In the following reviews the restaurants have a price rating, based on the average price of a main course per head excluding drinks.

£ - under €9
££ - €9-13
£££ - €13-17
££££ - €18-21
£££££ - over €21

Courchevel's **après** and **nightlife** is also one of extremes - and contrary to popular belief it is not just made up of dilettantes and debutantes. Don't expect to find the table-dancing antics of the Austrian resorts, but it's easy to get a cocktail or an overpriced 1664. There isn't much après on the mountain (probably because of the north-facing slopes). As nearly all of the hotels in 1850 have their own bars, the choice of 'independent' bars is fairly limited. Piano bars in particular abound - Alpes hôtel du Pralong, Byblos, Carlina, Chabichou, l'hôtel des Neiges, Les Ducs de Savoie, Les Grandes Alpes, Kilimandjaro, Lana, Pomme de Pin, Sivolière... the play list goes on. The après scene can be a little unpredictable. In busy weeks everywhere is busy, but conversely in quiet weeks you may struggle to find anyone anywhere. But with watering holes (outside of hotels) reasonably few and far between per head of population there isn't much space in the bar, so you may still have to elbow a fellow skier out of the way to get your beer.

snapshot

the best

The ingredients of most people's ideal ski holiday are pretty easy to pin down. You need mountains, and snow, good company, friendly locals, hearty après, stodgy food, some late night revelry and an early morning headache. Accordingly, along with being in the right location, ski resorts tend to provide liberal doses of fondue and beer and let your holiday spirit organise the rest. If you like to go home in the knowledge you've been to the best the area has to offer read on...

To start the day there's little to beat a hot pain au raisin or a chocolat croissant from one of the valley's many boulangeries - the excellent Gandy bakery has 3 outlets, and the one in 1850's Forum even has seating if you object to eating and moving at the same time.

The best restaurants for dinner are found at the extremes of the valley - 1850 and Le Praz. If you will only be placated by Michelin stars, 1850 has 2 such stellar restaurants - **le chabichou** (t 0479 0800555) in the hotel of the same name and **le bateau ivre** (t 0479 083688) in the hotel Pomme de Pin. At the first you can expect to dine on crayfish, frogs legs, spider crab and lobster where the latter dishes up a mean vension or foie gras. The typical Savoyarde experience is best sampled at **la fromagerie** in 1850 or **l'eterlou** in 1650. **l'oeil du boeuf** in 1550 serves up some excellent steak in a fire-warmed setting, **la cloche** in 1850 is a very good and very authentic French restaurant, and **le ya-ca** in Le Praz is a mini delight of *bon accueil* and well-cooked and delicious food. For as many incarnations of foie gras as there are months in the year make a booking at **le bistrot de praz**. For something to fill the gap between lunch and dinner **crêpancakes** in 1650 offers a delicious range of sweet and savoury crêpes to eat-in or take-away.

If you're more concerned with drinking, the most typical English après can be found at **le jump** in 1850, probably the best place for too much beer, and also the best spot to snuggle up with the English newspapers. For an equally friendly English welcome in 1650 the **bubble bar** is the best spot, and in La Tania the **pub le ski lodge**. To celebrate the French talent for making fine wine, **le chai des chartrons** in 1850 has the widest selection. For something as French but a little less refined **l'arbate** in La Tania is friendly. The best of the late night action depends upon your level of sophistication - **kalico's** in 1850 is the seasonnaire option while **les caves** offers something for the more refined.

courchevel 1850

As you approach the entrance of 1850, you could be forgiven for thinking the hype is wrong. The Porte (door) de Courchevel is far from pretty and 2 of the main buildings in the heart of the resort - the Croisette and the Forum - don't help. The Croisette is very much the centre of the resort - and where you will find the tourist office, the ESF, the post office, the main lift pass office and the 3 main lifts (the Jardin Alpin, Chenus and Verdons gondolas) up the mountain. The Forum is home to a number of commerces, including a supermarket, and a range of facilities from an ice-rink to a climbing wall. Just round the corner from the Croisette the charm of 1850 is more apparent - in the small stone church on and the wooden galleried shop fronts. And more often than not the streets are covered in snow which just adds to the general appeal. Something else that is more apparent away from the centre is the St.Tropez-on-Snow tag - palatial chalets line the road up the Altiport and it is worth a trip just to wow at Millionaires Row. The extremes of the village can be reached by bus. 4 services run from the Croisette - 1 to the Altiport, 1 to the Jardin Alpin, 1 to Chenus and 1 to Bellecôte, the frequency depending upon the destination. A one-way road system means that if you get lost in a car you may find yourself taking a circuitous tour of the village. Most of the restaurants and bars are based in the commercial centre, so those staying

further up the resort have the choice of eating in a hotel or walking (or taking a taxi) into town - one way to work up an appetite. Courchevel has something of a Conranesque empire - a number of the restaurants, hotels and shops (including the Hussard, the Grand Café, La Locomotive, L'Anerie, Le Café de la Poste, Cap Horn, La Cloche, La Grange, St. Joseph, Lana and the S'no Limit board store) are owned by the same family. For the more splendid restaurants it is a good idea to book. For access to the skiing 1850 is undoutedly the best placed of the resorts. Its season tends to start a week before the others and with such a conglomoration of lifts going in all directions, all pistes in the valley are easy to reach, as is the Méribel valley. In summary, while the resort has its detractors - and your bank manager is never going to be too happy that you ski there - it is difficult to think of something that it lacks.

90

copyright qanuk 2004

restaurants
1 la fromagerie
2 l'anerie
3 le refuge
4 le smalto
5 le planté du baton
6 le tremplin
7 la crêperie du moulin
8 la cloche
9 the end café
10 la basha
11 le hussard

cafés/take-away
12 le chocolathé
13 le saint honoré
14 la vache qui skie

bars
15 les 3 gringos
16 le chai des chartrons
17 isba
18 tj's
19 piggys'
20 prends ta luge et tire-toi
21 the jump

nightclubs
22 le kalico

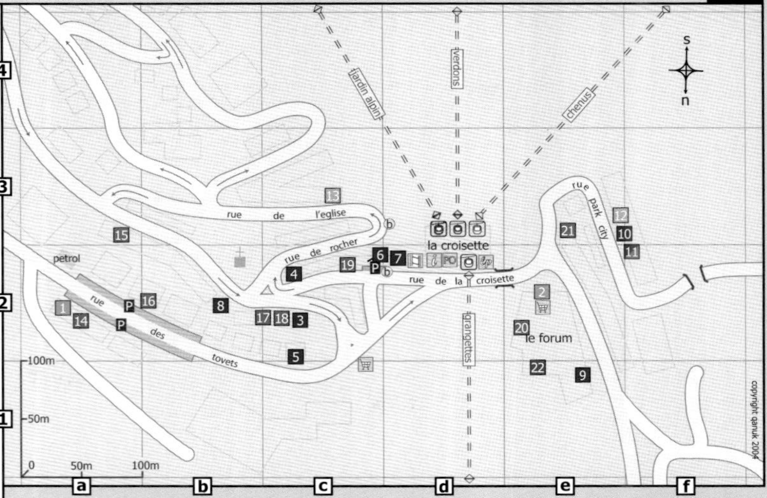

Map labels:
rue Park city
rue de la croisette
la croisette
rue de l'église
rue de rocher
rue de
rue des tovets
rue des
le forum
grangettes
verdons
jardin alpin
onvalz
petrol
N S W E
100m 50m 0
100m 50m

91

<< eating out >>

le hussard £££ £

p91
e/f2

☎ 0479 083837
🕐 7pm-11:30pm
✕ italian

Though it is situated on the ground floor of the hotel St. Joseph, Le Hussard is far too intimate to be categorised as just a hotel restaurant. Attention to detail in the décor has created a delightfully furnished and cosy setting - you feel like you are dining in a wealthy friend's dining room, which justifies the byline of Courchevel's "only lounge restaurant". Though not a cheap place to eat, the excellently presented and above all delicious Italian cuisine will give you little to grumble about.

le tremplin £££

p91
c/d2

☎ 0479 080619
🕐 12pm-4pm, 7pm-10:30pm
✕ seafood

The Tremplin (or Springboard) benefits from being the most prominent restaurant in the resort - next door to the Croisette overlooking the bottom of the pistes. Despite this, it is nearly always possible to get a table - either on the huge terrace at the front or in the sizeable seating area inside. And with its glass frontage and leather-bound booth seating, it resembles a Parisian brasserie. For lunch there are 2 daily menus and a

plat du jour. Evenings are more subdued and more expensive. While some of the menus are reasonably priced, if your heart is set on a seafood platter be prepared to pay in the environs of €100. And after that you're unlikely to be able to take-off.

le refuge ££

p91
c2

☎ 0479
🕐 11pm-11:30pm
✕ international

Le Refuge provides just that - an oasis of good, well-priced food in a veritable desert of expensive, traditional fare. Typical dishes include beef stroganoff and Thai curry, all served in a relaxed and friendly setting. Book your table during peak weeks as it only has room for 30 covers. It's also a laid-back place for some quiet après - and serves possibly the best (and certainly the biggest) hot chocolate in the valley.

le smalto ££

p91
c2

☎ 0479 083129
🕐 12pm-10:30pm
✕ pizza & pasta

Smalto serves a well-priced range of pizza and pasta dishes aimed at filling up the family without draining the wallet - the plat du jour comes in under the €15 bracket - though if you don't fancy a carbohydrate overload you can have a Savoyarde speciality. A brightly lit eaterie, the leather banquettes make for comfy dining and with its smiling waitresses, it's a cheery place for a relaxed evening meal.

l'anerie £££

☎ 0479 082915
🕐 12pm-3pm, 7pm-11pm
🍴 traditional savoyarde

Sharing an entrance with the neighbouring and similarly owned Locomotive, L'Anerie is a very different venture, offering traditional Savoyard fare in a suitably decorated setting - and is one of few restaurants in 1850 to offer pierre chaudes ('hot stones'). Based on the first floor, it has a large sunny terrace, open at lunch-time, from where you can enjoy your food whilst watching the action (and calamities) on the pistes.

la fromagerie £££

☎ 0479 082747
🕐 6:45pm-12:30am
🍴 cheese

This is the place (the clue being in the name) in 1850 for fondue and raclette - it serves quite a bewildering array of cheese-based dishes for both lunch and dinner. And though there is a small selection of fromageless options, if you're after a dairy-free meal you're better going elsewhere. With an eye on the late-dining market La Fromagerie is open until 12:30am and large groups are welcome.

la basha £££

☎ 0479 082891
🕐 6pm-11pm
🍴 asian

Basha offers Oriental-inspired cooking served to chill out music in lounge-style surroundings. The wine list is as big as the food menu, and later on drinking takes over from eating as restaurant becomes bar. Those looking for privacy should reserve the curtained VIP booth. But if you object to paying over £10 for what is effectively a plate of (admittedly very good) noodles, you might want to find somewhere else to dine.

93

la cloche £££

☎ 0479 083130
🕐 12pm-2:30pm, 7pm-11pm
🍴 classic french

Deservedly popular with locals and visitors alike, La Cloche serves up classic French fare - escargots, foie gras, scallops and veal - at reasonable prices (for 1850). Though the place settings seem a little formal, the décor of the small dining room is more rustic in style invoking memories of the past Alpine age and achieves a *"chaleureuse"* atmosphere. Lunch can be taken on the small terrace at the front overlooking the church (and clock). As seating is limited it is a good idea to book long before you hear the dinner bell.

courchevel 1850

the end café ££

☎ 0479 082042
🕐 8am-11pm
🍽 pizza

p91 e1 9

Probably the cheapest sit-down eats in the resort. The lower prices make for a mixed bag of clientele of young (children and resort workers) and old (locals) priced out of the other restaurants in the resort - which makes for an altogether un-1850 dining experience. The bulk of the menu is pizza, though breakfast (which is not pizza) is served until 11am, after which the lunch service starts. The namesake take-away is opposite and is your best option for late-night pizza as well as salads, crêpes and sandwiches.

le planté du baton ££

☎ 0479 080210
🕐 7pm-1am
🍽 local

p91 c2 5

Part-bar/part-restaurant, Le Planté du Bâton is very much a venue of 2 halves. Stepping into the restaurant is a little like stepping back in time - old sepia portraits, copper kitchenware, and curiously the occasional once-live cow. The bar is altogether more casual and offers lone diners or small groups a more relaxed setting - you can eat off the main menu in the bar - or if your mouth needs little more than amusement, tapas with a french twist is available. Le Planté is the

only place to offer burgers in the evening.

le chocolathé £

☎ 0479 010866
🕐 8am-6pm
🍽 teas & coffees

p91 e3

This delightful tea-room on Rue Park-City serves the very best of the hot beverage world - including teas from the Paris-based Mariage Frères and Illy coffee. The hot chocolate and the house speciality *"jus de pomme chaud à la cannelle"* - a hot cinnamon-spiced apple drink - aren't bad either. Though it is the most cosy of the (chocola)tea rooms the unjustifiably high prices may make you think twice about getting too comfortable - or even ordering a second cup.

le saint honoré £

☎ 0479 080202
🕐 8am-6:30pm
🍽 cake

p91 c3

Overlooking the Croisette and the end of the Bellecôte pistes, Le Saint Honoré (on the ground floor of the Hôtel des Grandes Alpes) is a great vantage spot for people-watching while taking tea. While the smartly dressed waiting staff make for a formal atmosphere and the stiff backed chairs are more suitable for posture improvement than languid lounging, you should be too distracted by the choice of cake - or the antics outside - to care.

94

le crêperie du moulin £££

p91
d2

☎ 0479 081090
🕐 8:30am-11pm
🍴 pancakes

The hipper and smaller sister of its (next door) neighbour Le Tremplin, Le Moulin is the choice in the resort for galettes and crêpes. All are delicious, particularly the wicked chocolate and banana for pud, and a wide choice of both savoury and sweet is available, though for the pleasure of sitting down you pay twice the price you pay at the nearby grand marnier take-away. The Mill is one of the few places you can eat at any time of the day - it serves a continental breakfast from 8:30am so keen skiers can munch on a croissant whilst waiting for the lifts to open.

la vache qui skie £

p91
a2

☎ -
🕐 10pm-5:30am
🍴 burgers & paninis

Given the overriding image of style and sophistication that 1850 portrays, it is probably the last place you expect to find a kebab shop. And whilst the cow that skis does not offer the same dubious 'delicacies' as your local, it should manage to calm a rumbling tummy. With an up-market slant on the kebab - paninis are served rather than doners - and it is the only place open late if the midnight munchies can't be ignored.

and the rest

The choice is far from ending there - if none of those tickle your tastebuds. At **le bistrot de la mangeoire** (t 0479 080209) you eat to musical accompaniment. **la saulire** (t 0479 080752) is another good option for fish and seafood while **la cendrée** (t 0479 082938) caters for Italian preferences, serving up the ubiquitious pizza and pasta dishes as well as more traditional offerings such as carpaccio de boeuf. Arguably the best option for a take-away lunch is **chez le gaulois** (t 0479 080399) at the entrance to the Forum - or the branch in 1650. The choice is limited, but when it's jambon cru and hot raclette cheese, it's difficult enough to make - hot, satisfying and a snip at €5 a go. **show pain** on the middle level of the Forum (and the sit-down branch of the Gandy bakeries) offers a range of less regional sandwiches, hot drinks and mouth-watering cakes and pastries - and unlike other boulangeries it doesn't shut for lunch. For those staying on the Bellecôte side of the village, **l'oriental** at the hotel Byblos provides a welcome - albeit expensive - change from cheese. Those staying on the Chenus side will have to go into town for dinner - though they may be seduced by the **bateau ivre** or the **chabichou** on the way down. For crêpes on the hoof, the **grand marnier** (t 0479 080075) outlet is not for those who have taken the Pledge - all are doused with the name-sake liqueur.

95

<< après ski & nightlife >>

le jump

☎ 0479 080900
🕐 9:30am-1am

English-run and English-frequented, Le Jump just needs an ing after its name. The closest you'll get to a pub, and even then one along more modern lines - from the light wood furniture to the lunchtime menu of salads, sandwiches and pasta. At 5pm, the stampede of refreshment seekers - mainly seasonnaires and (newly-made) friends - descend to make merry après and though English newspapers are available to read you'll be lucky to find enough peace or elbow room to read them.

prends ta luge et tire-toi

☎ 0479 087868
🕐 10am-1am

A cool little corner in the board shop of the same name. A well-designed space, the backdrop to the groaning shelves of the bar is a wall of TV screens showing MTV or extreme videos - so it's easy for 1 coffee to become more. You can also check your email. During the day the menu offers reasonable burgers and paninis, while in the evening it becomes a bar - its rum corner being particularly popular with French seasonnaires - and is where you head if you want to chew the cud in French over a Gauloise and a 1664.

le piggys'

☎ 0479 080071
🕐 5pm-1am

Piggys' appearance is somewhat deceptive. The red and windowless exterior suggests an Irish bar, which couldn't be further from the baroque-themed interior with its coved ceiling and heraldic ensigns. True, they serve Guinness on draught, but they also serve (expensive) cocktails and it's certainly not the (Irish) norm to down your pint with caviar or foie gras. Live bands play most evenings though the closeness of the stage to the seating can make it a little too cosy - or the ideal venue for the hard of hearing.

le chai des chartrons

☎ 0479 003653
🕐 5pm-1am

1850's hidden après gem - in real terms because of its subterranean location and otherwise because it is little known among the English contingent and doesn't form part of most people's evening excursions. In this lovely cellar you can work your way through a well-chosen menu of grape-based delights - and the genial maître d' will recommend one if you're thrown by the menu. Light snacks are available - such as foie gras and escargots. And if any of the tipples takes your fancy you can buy them from the wine shop on the floor above.

96

tj's

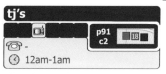

☎ -
🕐 12am-1am

p91
c2 ▦ 18

TJ's is about as far away from the 'Chai' as Australia is from England - you're unlikely to find a local here or more than a couple of choices of wine, though the range of lurid vodkas and shooters is extensive. One of 3 bars under the same British management - the others are the 3 Gringos slightly further up the hill and the Isba just next door - this is the most popular of the 3, in part because of its location and in part due to the warm welcome you will receive. And the place to go to get you in the mood for a party.

le kalico

☎ 0479 082028
🕐 10am-4am

p91
e1 ▦ 22

Though Le Kalico does serve food, its main claim to fame is as a night-spot for the energetically unchallenged. Based slope-side on the lowest floor of the Forum it comes into its own at dance o'clock - though if you've dined in the restaurant during the day (burgers 12pm-3pm and tex-mex 7pm-10pm) it can be a little unnerving to find yourself dancing where you last ate enchiladas. The vibe is youthful - the bulk of the clientele falling into the "18-30" bracket - the music is pop and the drinking is non-stop.

and the rest

If you can't face the crowds at the Jump and don't want to wander too far looking for an alternative, the tiny bar in the **s'no limit** board shop next door is a favourite with French ski instructors for early après. Later on the **3 gringos** is the other bar of choice for seasonnaires, with cheap prices but short opening hours - before it opens its clientele can be found in the **isba** which apart from its airport lounge appearance more than adequately fills the gap. Otherwise the choice is limited to the hotel bars - that at the **mélézin** is one of the most chic (and the most expensive), while that at **les tovets** is pared-down simplicity in menu and style. Or try one of the numerous piano bars. Restaurants such as **le tremplin**, **le moulin** and **le planté du bâton** will happily welcome you in for just a drink. For other late-night options - or rather early morning, as they stay open until 4am - **les caves** (t 0479 081274) at the Porte du Courchevel is where you will find most of the beautiful people after the rest have turned into pumpkins. **les nuits de bacchus** (t 0479 082962) serves food until closing time as does the North African-themed **la grange** (t 0479 081461) on Rue Park-City which has a pleasingly late happy hour (11pm-1am). Both Les Caves and Les Nuits have regular cabaret shows should you want to be entertained.

97

courchevel 1650

1650, or Moriond, is the Courchevel choice for those wanting to stay at altitude without paying sky-high prices. Much smaller than 1850, the majority of 1650 is concentrated along the main road up the mountain - a road-side sprawl of shops, restaurants and bars. Part of the façade of the resort - that can be seen from the road as you approach the resort - is undergoing some change. The blocky, but much-loved, Signal hotel and bar had its last season in 2004 and is being replaced by an altogether prettier development - the

chalet style Le Seizena. For many the Signal was the heart and soul of the resort and it remains to be seen whether its replacement will prove such a gathering hole for Mutzig drinking locals - and it leaves the community of seasonnaires looking for a new home from home. Elsewhere the sky-line is dominated by multi-storey apartments blocks, which provide the bulk of the accommodation - the rest is found in 3* hotels, tour operator run chalet-hotels and low-rise chalets. These architectural monstrosities belie that the commercial centre of the resort, the Rue de Marquis found just off the main roundabout, is actually quite attractive and has far more soul than 1850. The resort has all the usual suspects for equipment rental - the France-wide Intersport and Twinner - as well as the well regarded and British-run Freeride, and for boarders branches of S'no Limit and Endless Winter. The New Generation ski school is based here

and there is significant representation from the ESF. There are 2 lift pass offices - one in the centre at the top of the escalator, which links the resort to the lift links and pistes, and one by the bottom of the 3 Vallées chairlift, on the edge of the town. At the bottom of the escalator you will find the friendly tourist office and the easy-to-miss chapel, which is worth a visit - whether you need to find divine inspiration to help your ski technique or simply to see the beautiful stained-glass windows inside. The significant presence of UK tour operators - and consequently UK hoilday-makers - means the bars are seldom quiet as fun-seeking crowds gather for après and general fun. Locals are also a more common sight here than further up the road and the resort is also brought to life twice a week by a local market. Somehow this all combines to make an enjoyable mélange of ski tourism and mountain authenticity.

98

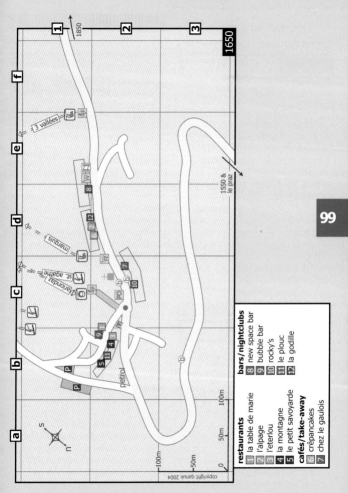

restaurants
1. la table de marie
2. l'alpage
3. 'eteriou
4. la montagne
5. le petit savoyarde

cafés/take-away
6. crépancakes
7. chez le gaulois

bars/nightclubs
8. new space bar
9. bubble bar
10. rocky's
11. le plouc
12. la godille

99

1850

1650

1550 & le praz

3 vallées

marquis

st. agathe

arondaz

petrol

100m

50m

0

100m

50m

copyright qanuk 2004

n s

<< eating out >>

l'eterlou £££

☎ 0479 082545
🕐 12pm-2:30pm, 7pm-10:30pm
🍴 savoyarde

A favourite among locals and regulars to the resort, L'Eterlou is a charming little restaurant on the Rue du Marquis, just past the Freeride shop. Savoyarde in style and Savoyarde in menu, all the regional favourites are on offer - braserade, reblochonnade and a tasty tartichèvre (similar to tartiflette but with goat's cheese). A good place to take the family - a children's menu is available - and bookings are essential on 'chalet night off' as this is the first restaurant to fill up. During the day lunch can be taken on the small terrace at the front.

100

le petit savoyarde £££

☎ 0479 082744
🕐 12pm-2pm, 7pm-10:30pm
🍴 savoyarde & pizza

While you can of course have a fondue at Le Petit Savoyarde, the pizza menu is the main reason to go, despite the name. Their disc-shaped dishes are cooked to perfection in a wood-fired oven and are large enough to feed a small family. If you have room at lunchtime, the best choice is normally the well-priced main course and pud combo. A well-lit and charmingly decorated space, it ticks all the boxes for an enjoyable dining experience.

crepancakes £

☎ 0479 089553
🕐 8am-10pm
🍴 crêpes

Break down the name and you can work out what's on offer at the cleverly titled Crêpancakes. A sweet little café, it is open before the lifts so you can breakfast on pancakes or *'le petit-déjeuners anglo-saxons'*. Lunch too can be pancake based, as can afternoon tea, or an early supper and if you are in a hurry you can take away too. Those with a sweet tooth will delight in the chocolate fondues, and those without can settle for a sandwich.

and the rest

le table de marie (t 0479 011897) on Rue de Marquis is another option for a cheesy meal - though most will try to get into L'Eterlou first - and **l'alpage** (t 0479 082487) is similar, and more convenient for those staying at the upper end of the resort. The menu at **la montagne** (t 0479 080985) is not restricted to Savoyarde staples but includes some tasty meat and fish options. For lunch, as in 1850, it is hard to beat the hot cheese and ham sandwiches from **chez le gaulois** - and if you have room a cake from the **gandy boulangerie**. Fill the fridge in case of midnight munchies - or be prepared to make your way to 1850.

<< après ski & nightlife >>

bubble bar

☎ 0479 011421
🕐 8am-1am

A fairly recent addition to the resort, the Bubble is a modern space that is as much of a daytime hangout as it is an evening drinking venue. With internet terminals, comfy sofas, a snack menu, English newspapers and films (on bad weather days) it can be difficult to persuade yourself to get on the slopes and before you know it you're tucking into an early evening cocktail. Always something of a seasonnaire hang-out, their numbers are likely to increase with the closure of the Signal bar - but it makes for a party atmosphere particularly during the "double bubble" happy hour.

le plouc

☎ -
🕐 12pm-1am

A tiny *bar à vin* on the Rue de Marquis that resembles somewhere you'd find in a provincial French town. It is the place you should head if you're keen to meet a real live local or a real and lively ski instructor and consequently has a more authentic feel than the resort's other bars (perhaps also because it is not run by an English tour operator). Just remember to order your *pression* in your best schoolboy French.

rocky's bar

☎ -
🕐 10am-1am

Run by the UK tour operator Ski Olympic (who also run the Les Avals chalet-hotel upstairs), Rocky's attracts an eclectic mix, from old-timers to fresh-faced seasonnaires. Like its clientele it is a place of many different faces - on the one hand, a laid-back place to sip on a hot chocolate and take in the last rays of the day and on the other, somewhere for a hooly helped along by any number of interestingly flavoured vodkas. Whatever rocks your boat you should be able to find it here.

101

and the rest

To continue your evening into the morning, you are limited to the **new space bar** (t 0479 082375) or **la godille** (t 0479 083975). The former, just below the cinema, could as well be called the big space bar as it is somewhat cavernous in feel. All things to all people, you can enjoy the live bands that play here regularly, watch an extreme video or just set the world to rights over a quiet beer. At the latter dancing is the main activity on the agenda. At either you needn't think about bed before 4am.

Often the forgotten cousin, 1550 is the original Courchevel and the last resort to be reached by new investment. The next few years should see the regeneration of the rather tired looking blocks of accommodation and wooden-fronted commerces - the first instalment is the lovely Le Hameau enclave of chalets, and 2 of the lifts from the snow front have been upgraded for 2004. A good choice for families, while it lacks the glamour of 1850 and the friendly soul of 1650 it has everything else you could conceivably need.

102

<< eating out >>

l'oeil du boeuf £££

☎ 0479 082210
🕐 12pm-3:30am, 7pm-11pm
🍴 traditional & savoyarde

L'Oeil is one of the valley's culinary highlights, serving the best steak you will find. A cosy little wooden cabin across from the bottom of the pistes, its location and cuisine make it a popular venue for the ESF's instructors to idle away their free time. Most of the food on the menu is ember grilled over the open fire - and with 40 years of practice you won't be disappointed - and you can eat inside or on the sun warmed terrace. And while the ever-watchful Ox's Eye can be a little disconcerting as you munch your way through the best part of a cow, the atmosphere and excellent food will soon help you forget.

<< après ski & nightlife >>

le barouf

☎ 0479 080471
🕐 12pm-1:30am

The relatively youthful Barouf is the hub of nightlife in 1550 and more the makes up for the otherwise quiet après scene. With a kitchen sink approach to entertainment, you can start the evening with a quiet vin chaud or coffee while watching the latest sporting fixtures. Later on such serenity gives way to more serious drinking and the bar lives up to its name (barouf = a din) when more often than not live music or a seasonnaire-attended theme night generates a party atmosphere.

and the rest

For less-meaty dining **le cortona** (t 0479 080487) offers tagliatelle "10 ways" and over 20 pizzas (cooked *au feu de bois*) while **le caveau** (t 0479 080942) is the choice for cheese-based Savoyarde dishes in a rustic setting. For snacky food **la normandise** (t 0479 081618) dishes up decent crêpes. Apart from the Barouf the other choices for drinking are the tour operator run **the bar** (Pleisure) - a good place to chill out - or **jackson's** (Ski Olympic) which offers more robust après. The French-run **la taverne** is a pleasant place to while away the late afternoon.

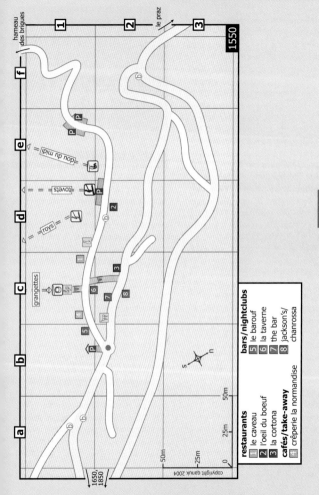

103

1550

hameau des brigues

le praz

restaurants
1. le caveau
2. l'oeil du boeuf
3. la cortona

cafés/take-away
4. crêperie la normandise

bars/nightclubs
5. le barouf
6. la taverne
7. the bar
8. jackson's/chanrossa

grangettes

rots

tovets

du midi

1650, 1850

50m   25m   0

50m   25m

copyright ganuk 2004

le praz

A small, traditional and picturesque village sitting at 1300m, Le Praz is the lowest of the resorts to receive winter visitors. Sitting at the crossroads between La Tania and the 1550, 1650 and 1850 resorts, though it is easy to miss the village as you drive up the hill in search of the snowline this is the place for the most French experience on this side of Les Trois Vallées. It is also the most peaceful (some would say subdued) of the Courchevel resorts. Similar to Méribel's Les Allues in Le Praz you will find the perennial population, a friendly mix of French and English people. And though the village is small, its year-round existence explains the presence of a post office (open during the week 2pm-5pm), a church, a doctor, a cashpoint, a library, a museum, a newsagent, a small but good supermarket (selling fruit, veg, fresh bread and cheese, open 8am-12pm, 4:30pm-7pm) and a few ski rental shops. A favourite with families, various tour operator run crèches are based in the village, meaning the average height of the seasonal population is about 1 metre.

The resort has 2 hearts - one is the village square on which sits Les Peupliers hotel and a few other commerces. The square is at its best during March and April, when the warm spring sunshine can make you forget that there is still skiing to be done just a few hundred metres up the hill. A couple of cobbled streets away is the

more modern and functional Galerie d'Or - a gallery of shops where you can buy your daily paper, send your postcards and do some washing. Across the road from the village is the main lift station, a small tourist office, the lift pass, cross-country and ESF offices, and the village kindergarten. The right edge of the village is dominated by the ski jump, which was built for the 1992 Olympics and which is still used for competitions.

Le Praz is well linked to the skiing by 2 gondolas - one runs to mid-way up the mountain, to the collection of slopes at the western edge of the Courchevel valley, while the other links the village to 1850. The gondolas also provide the way home when poor snow conditions prevent you from skiing down.

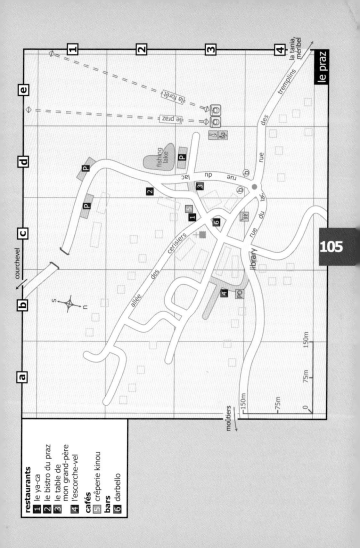

restaurants
1. le ya-ca
2. le bistro du praz
3. le table de mon grand-père
4. l'escorche-vel

cafés
5. crêperie kinou

bars
6. darbello

le praz

courchevel

la tania, méribel

moûtiers

fishing lake

= la forêt

= le praz

rue des tremplins

rue du lac

rue du lac

allée des cerisiers

library

−150m   −75m   0   75m   150m

150m   75m

le praz

<< eating out >>

le bistro du praz ££££

☎ 0479 084133
🕐 12pm-2:30pm, 7pm-10:30pm
🍴 classic french & foie gras

Le Bistrot du Praz is the valley's low-level culinary star - and with 12 types of foie gras (the house speciality) you can be sure it earns its price tag. The wine list has enough choices that you'll find one to go with each, and then some. Though some find the atmosphere a little too French - and the restaurant has something of a reputation for gastro-snobbery - others will delight in the welcome extended by its moustachioed patron, one of the most stylish hosts in the Alps. And don't worry if you fundamentally object to the whole concept of fatted-goose liver pâté, you can enjoy 4 types of carpaccio, and any number of delicious meat and fish-based dishes.

106

le ya-ca £££

☎ 0479 084104
🕐 7pm-11pm
🍴 traditional

A tiny place with a huge reputation, the unpronounceable and untranslatable Le Ya-Ca is a charming, family run restaurant with the appearance of a well decorated and comfortable living room. The food is traditional French cooking -

local produce is used in many of the dishes, and though the restaurant is tiny, the wine cellar is significantly bigger - with hundreds of bottles to choose from. Only open in the evening, you need to book no matter the size of your party.

crêperie kinou £

☎ 0479 084290
🕐 12pm-10pm
🍴 crêpes

Those looking for a snack (or just something within the holiday budget) should head to the Kinou. Both savoury (galettes) and sweet crêpes are available - good for lunch, or indeed any time of day - as well as tasty salads and irresistible desserts. The atmosphere is low-key and cheerful and this is somewhere you can happily while away the day with a good book - on ski technique, of course.

and the rest

For outdoor dining the main choice is **la table de mon grand-père** (t 0479 084142) in Les Peupliers hotel - its large patio on the main square makes it the perfect place to people-watch or to enjoy the spring sunshine.

<< après ski & nightlife >>

darbello

p105
c3   6

☎ -
🕐 12pm-1am

The Darbello bar/restaurant is tucked away behind Les Peupliers hotel. Go there during the day and you'll be charmed by its cosy and cavernous stone-clad interior and ever-smiling patron. Go back a bit later and you may think you're walked into an entirely different place - it is likely that the quiet ambience and handful of locals will have been replaced by a lively crowd, engaged in dining on the decent range of regional dishes or making good use of the extensive range of fire-waters. Live bands regularly play here - so if you are planning a quiet meal out check the gig list before you book.

l'escorche-vel

p105
b3   4

☎ 0479 084344
🕐 5pm-1:30am

The most typical ski resort après is found in L'Escorche-Vel in the gallery of shops at the centre of the resort. Though food is served in the evening - pizza, pasta and Savoyarde dishes are available - most people go for a beer and to enjoy the live bands that play regularly. You don't have to wait for dinner to eat - snacks are served during the late afternoon - and if you are hoping to watch your team playing their latest fixture, this is the only bar in town to show live sport.

and the rest

The newly-refurbished **norby's bar** in Les Peupliers hotel is the most civilised option for après. A delicious afternoon tea is served until early evening, though you can skip that for more liquid refreshment if you so desire.

107

la tania

Whilst La Tania does not have the infrastructure of the other Courchevel villages - with no bank or doctor (the nearest of both are in Le Praz) and a post office that is only sporadically open - it is self-sufficient in most other ways. There is a well-stocked Sherpa supermarket (which also does a good trade in rotisserie chickens), a (token) tourist office, restaurants, pubs, a newsagent, a lift pass office, a branch of the ESF, a booking office for Magic in Motion, a Maison des Enfants, a boulangerie and a fromagerie. The

rental shops range from the nationwide Ski Set chain, with a good range of skis and very friendly staff, to the English-run Ski Higher - a sister of the 1850 store and the same approach.

Set on 2 levels, the original resort is a development of medium-rise apartment blocks and a horse-shoe cluster of commerce around the bottom of the pistes. Car-free, it a safe place for children to play. And the short Troïka lift is ideal for children learning to ski - it starts in the village and leads to the top of a gentle green piste, which is only busy at the end of the skiing day when the the rest of La Tania's residents return home. To the left of the centre is an enclave of traditional-style chalets that sit prettily among the trees - many of which are run or managed by English tour operators. This upper section of the resort is reached by a lift up 9 floors through the Grand Bois apartments. The resort has a total of 4000 beds.

Although La Tania is only at 1400m, it is possible for almost the entire season to ski back to the village and in a large number of cases direct to your accommodation, along a series of tree-lined slopes. And the protection given by the surrounding forest means that when too much snow falls and the rest of the Courchevel valley is unreachable, the slopes around La Tania may well be open. Though the resort is closer to Méribel - and if you fancy a change of scene that resort is only 20 minutes away by road - than to the higher Courchevel villages of 1650 and 1850, the lift system from La Tania only links you to the skiing on the Courchevel side.

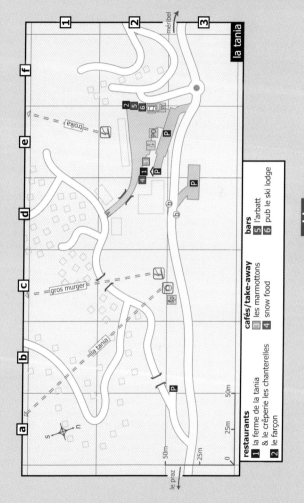

109

restaurants
1 la ferme de la tania
& le crêperie les chanterelles
2 le farçon

cafés/take-away
3 les marmottons
4 snow food

bars
5 l'arbatt
6 pub le ski lodge

méribel

troïka

gros murger

la tania

le praz

50m
25m
0
50m
25m

<< eating out >>

la ferme de la tania €€€

☎ 0479 082325
🕐 12pm-11pm
🍴 savoyarde specialities & crêpes

Two places in one - by day it is the more-café-than-restaurant Les Chanterelles (a crêperie) and by night the hat of more-restaurant-than-café La Ferme (a Savoyarde restaurant). Crêpes can be enjoyed on the large terrace outside and are also available to take-away. In the evening, the choice is fairly standard fondue, raclette and other regional dishes - but as prices are reasonable and tables are normally available it is a good option for families. And if you're not a family and don't want to join in the fun, you can take away raclette and tartiflette.

110

le farçon €€€€€

☎ 0479 088034
🕐 lunch & evening
🍴 haute cuisine

La Tania's gastronomic option - the food is more haute cuisine than high mountain hut. As the entrance to the restaurant is through the Arbatt pub, things get off to a unprepossessing start. However once you get past the *pression*-wielding locals and seasonnaires, the charming chalet-style room and the mouth-watering menu should reassure you. As will the food - dishes are well-cooked and carefully presented, and if you can't make a choice ask for the 'tasting menu' which takes away the need for a decision. Though Le Farçon is not cheap - and your wallet will leave feeling lighter - you will leave feeling fully satisified.

les marmottons €€

☎ 0479 088163
🕐 11am-10pm
🍴 pancakes & sandwiches

Though it shares similar features to Les Chanterelles - a sun-baked terrace and a wide menu of crêpes - Les Marmottons is an easier place to spend a bad weather day. A smaller place, the pine décor is somehow more authentic and the waiting staff more friendly. The menu also includes cakes, ice-cream, salads, pizzas (which are available to take-away), omelettes and Savoyarde specialities.

and the rest

The small **snow food** hatch (t 0479 084899) on the Front de Neige serves up sandwiches and paninis for those in a hurry - or you can grab a sandwich or cake (and English conserves!) from the **au delice de la source** bakery.

l'épicéa in the Jeunesse et Sports run Le Chalet du Sud (t 0479 088032/0612 119916) is the only restaurant in the upper section of the resort and is open to non-residents for Savoyarde dining.

<< après ski & nightlife >>

pub ski le lodge

☎ 0479 084899
🕐 10am-2am

p109
e2

For many the Pub Le Ski Lodge is the centre of La Tania's après scene - not least because it is the first place you notice (or rather hear). Heaven for some and hell for others, the formula is well-priced drinks, no-nonsense food (of the kind you would find on the menu in an English pub) and fun, fun, fun. The clientele is mainly English, as are the bar staff, the owners, the music and the sport on TV. Looking for a fancy dress theme night? You'll find it here, as well as live bands and lively seasonnaires. During the day drinks can be enjoyed on a large terrace at the front and at any time you can surf the internet whilst tucking into your jacket potato.

l'arbatt

☎ -
🕐 12pm-1:30am

p109
e/f2

For those who regard the Englishness of the Lodge with dismay, the more French L'Arbatt may well provide welcome respite. Though the two couldn't be closer in location they are worlds apart in style. Looking for a chance to brush up on your French vocab? Your best chance is here - as is the chance to practise your pool skills and to actually hear the conversation of your fellow drinkers. While L'Arbatt may not have Guinness on tap, you will find plenty of French lager and an extensive range of French liqueurs, and as it doesn't have a busy night as such, head here first if a seat is top of your priority list.

and the rest

The piano bar in the hotel **montana** is the last remaining option for après - and the closest thing to sophistication. And finally, night-owls beware - come 2am, all the shutters in the resort come down.

111

activities

When the lifts are closed because of too little or - more frustratingly - too much snow, there a few things to keep you occupied.

get some air

No surprise, it is easy to take to the skies in Courchevel. For a short **aeroplane** flight or lessons try any of: the Dauphine flying club (t 0479 083123, i aero-courchevel.com), Les 3 Vallées flying club (t 0662 248235/0479 002064) and Alpes Aviation (t 046 62 2482 35 - check). For **helicopter** tours contact s.a.f (t 0479 080091). **air balloon flights** - from ½ to 1 hour over the valley - are available through Aéro-action Adventure (t 0607 481679, i aero-action-aventure.com), weather permitting. There are a number of **parapenting** schools - though most 'flights' launch from the sunny Col de la Loze plateau. Contact any of Air Extreme (t 0671 902195), Air Performance (t 0689 813489), Craig's Paragliding (t 0479 084365/ 0681 646970, i paraglide-alps.com), Jean Jacques Dejouy (t 0479 082467/ 0609 911313), Delta Parapente Club (t 0662 064613), Ski Vol (t 0479 084172, i www.skivol.com). For the last 3 activities you are at the mercy of the elements, so remember to wrap up warm!

112

bad weather days

There are **cinemas** in 1850 - Le Terminal (t 0479 080019) and Le Tremplin (t 0479 082239) - and in 1650 (t 0479 082510). Look for films marked VOST (*Version Originale*) for English language films. There are normally 2 screenings a day (5.30 and 9pm and an extra showing at 2.30pm in bad weather), with an equal mix of French and English films. There is also a cineam in La Tania (t 0479 084040) but showings are limited to Mondays and Thursdays at 6pm in French during the school holidays.

The basement of the Forum is the salvation of many a stressed parent when skiing is not an option. Activities on offer include **bowling** (t 0479 082383), a **salle de jeux** and a **climbing wall** (t 0479 081950). Hungry parents can eat at the on-site restaurant, which serves standard snack food 9am-2am, while their children play. The Forum also has an **ice-skating** rink (t 0479 083323) that is open for public skating and is host to the occasional hockey match.

chillin'

Many of the hotels have **spa** complexes which are open to non-residents, up in the Jardin Alpin area the Byblos (t 0479 082582) has one of the most luxurious. The Hotel des Grande Alpes (t 0479 080540) close to the Croisette has a **swimming pool** as well as a sauna and hammam - as does Le Lana (t 0479 080110) and the hotel Carlina (t 0479 080030). **massages** and **beauty treatments** are also available at most of them if you need some pampering. The Gym Club Med in the Forum is for those looking for a more strenuous work-out. For total non-activity contact **boutik services** (t 0609 580988, i boutik.services.free.fr) - a type of mobile concierge service they can arrange food delivery (be it groceries or an à la carte meal), TV and video rental and even find you a Christmas tree.

credit-card bashing

Though some people come to

Courchevel to ski, it seems many come just to **shop**. In 1850 the range of commerces is extensive, from the galleries of designer boutiques where nothing is cheap to the bi-weekly streetmarket on the street for bargain fleeces and local produce. Should you be looking to kit yourself out, re-decorate your living room, add to your art collection or simply buy a present for granny there are shops for all. The lower resorts have a more ski-resort typical range of sports stores and souvenir shops.

Though the resort does not have a casino you can **bet** your change away at the PMU in the hotel Potinière, just opposite the entrance to the Forum and where you will find a number of the locals.

113

learn something new

The hotel Chabichou goes to the top of the class for providing educational alternatives. From time to time the Michelin-starred Michel Rochedy runs **cookery** classes and there is a regular **bridge** club. Elsewhere you can join a cultural tour of Courchevel (t 0479 605900, i savoie-patrimoine.com) or pay a visit to the Olympic ski jump in Le Praz (t 0479 081950). Even further afield (in Moûtiers) you can pay a visit to one of the local **cheesemakers** (t 0479 240365) and see how the main ingredient in your fondue gets made.

The 3 Vallées is one of the best areas to go skiing with children. Courchevel is one of the 57 French resorts to have been awarded the P'tit Montagnards status - this indicates that the resort is suitable for families and children on the basis of 9 criteria. Because of the valley's popularity with families, it is essential to book what you need - particularly nurseries, ski lessons and equipment before you arrive (1850 has been known to run out children's skis in peak weeks!).

tour operators

114

ski scott dunn is the leader of the childcare programme pack in 1850. It runs a dedicated ski school for children over the school holidays (Christmas/New Year, February half term and Easter), in association with Ski Academy. Children (aged 4-10 years) are split into 4 different groups according to ability. Outside of skiing, they have private nannies to look after children staying in their chalets (from 6 months upwards - a service which must be booked before departure), as well as a children's club (6 months-6 years). This is run in one of the chalets and is for non-skiing children or those not old enough to join ski school. Children are picked up in the morning (9am) and delivered back in the evening (5pm) every day except Sunday. Lower down the hill in Le Praz **esprit ski** runs an extensive childcare programme - nannies and small tots wearing logoed bibs are a common sight among the cobbled streets of the village. The British-run nanny service **snow kidz** (t 0870 402 8888, i snow kidz.com) will arrange childcare at your chalet - all nannies are British and have the relevant qualifications. The service is available Sundays-Fridays 9am-5pm, and you can also arrange evening babysitting through them. Nannies work to the ratio of 1:2 for children under 2 years and 1:3 for children over 3 years.

in-resort

There are 2 **kindergartens** for children aged 18 months-12 years (open every day 9am-5pm). Lunch is available. **le village des enfants** (t 0479 080847, i esfcourchevel.com) in 1850 is located close to the Forum. A ESF run day-nursery it provides indoor and outdoor activities for a half day morning (9am-12pm) and afternoon (2:15pm-4:30pm), under the responsibility of qualified instructors. Lunch is also available and the price includes a lift pass. **les pitchounets** (t 0479 083369, i esfcourchevel1650.com) in 1650 is located at the foot of the runs and has a specially reserved play area for children. Open 9am-5pm, children above the age of 18 months are welcome.

The tourist office, your hotel or apartment manager can put you in touch with qualified private **babysitters** who provide child care services at any time of the day or night. Jean-Louis Voisin (t 0620 663723) can also arrange baby-sitting 24 hours a day 7 days a week. **kids etcetera** (t 0479 007139/0622 626903 (mobile), i kidsetc.co.uk) is a well established and trusted organisation run by a Brit, which provides childcare to families staying in La Tania. All the nannies have the necessary childcare qualifications, and they are available to look after children of all ages on a private or playgroups basis, during the day or evening.

Of the five ESF **schools** in the valley, the one in 1550 has the best reputation for childrens' lessons - it has a Club des Piou-Piou for children aged 3-5, 9:15am-4:30pm and runs standard group lessons for children aged 6-12 or slightly more expensive group lessons for "very important children" - class size is restricted to 6. They have meeting points in 1850 as well so can be used by those staying up there, though the 1850 ESF also runs standard group ski lessons for children aged 3-12 years and above departing from the Croisette as well as courses for more advanced skiers (aged 7-12). In 1650 the Club des Oursons at the bottom of the pistes and based in a specially designed snow garden takes youngsters new to skiing aged 3 years and above - outside the school holidays this is also open at weekends. Otherwise the same ski and snowboard group lessons are available for 5 or 6 days, 6 mornings or 6 afternoons - or you can opt for the "tout compris" package which includes lessons, lunch and lift pass. The ESF in

La Tania has a crèche, which takes children from 3 years up for half or full days with lunch as an option. There is also a Jardin des Neiges for 4-12 year olds where ESF instructors teach children to ski in a special area. For any of the ESF group lessons it is compulsory to wear helmets. The other schools also run lessons for children. Magic in Motion run lessons for 4-6 years old and groups for children aged 6 and above - instruction is given in English. The Ski Academy takes children aged 4 or over every morning 9:30am-12:30pm. Older children or teenagers can join the Champion Ski Club (10-13 years) and the

Competition Club (14-16 years), while Supreme Ski runs groups lessons for children aged 6-12 years (during the school holidays only). You can save money by buying children's **lift passes** as part of a ski school package.

After the lifts close in 1850 (or when the weather closes in) parents with bored children on their hands need look little further than the basement of the Forum (➔ activities). In 1650 the ESF run an evening on special events on Wednesdays which includes a torchlit descent for children. In 1850 the 2kms toboggan run to 1550 is open 9am-7:30pm - and is floodlit at night. La Tania holds events for children throughout the season - at the family-focussed charity day towards the end of there is normally a BBQ, a fancy dress race, and other competitions.

before you go

Before you decide what kind of job you want you need to decide what kind of season you want - a job as a rep will be better paid but you have more responsibility, while a job as a chalet host means fixed hours, but once you know the routine, more time to make the most of resort life. Most of the UK ski companies recruit seasonal workers - interviewing normally starts in May, though there may still be vacancies as late as December. Either contact the companies directly (not forgetting smaller or overseas based ones) or go through a recruitment website such as **natives** (i natives.co.uk) who has a comprehensive database of available jobs as well as a lot of useful information on everything about "doing a season". It's a competitive market for jobs and while it is not essential, speaking reasonable French will help. If you haven't got a job by October, it's worth going to the Ski Show in London - some tour operators have a stall there as does Natives. If you haven't got a job by the start of the season, it can be worth heading out to the resort (if you can support yourself for a bit). Some of the less glamourous jobs may still be available and you will also get known - so when there is the inevitable fall-out of recruits due to unsuitability, New Year flu and mid-season blues, you can step into the role. Jobs constantly become available throughout the season - the ski market is very transient. Once

employed most companies organise your work permit, your travel to and from the resort, accommodation, lift pass and equipment rental. Most seasonnaire jobs come with a shared room as part of the package. If accommodation doesn't come with your job - or if you aren't planning on having a job - you would be well advised to find some digs before you head out. The seasonal accommodation situation in the Courchevel valley is one of the worst - seasonnaires can find themselves living as far away as Brides les Bains, because of limited availability and crippling prices. Only the lucky few (mainly live-in chalet staff) will find themselves living in 1850. More (and cheaper) apartment accommodation is located in 1650, 1550 and Le Praz. Tour operators in the lower resorts tend to be able to accommodate their workers nearby - so you have a better lifestyle! And if you live in any of the smaller resorts, you are likely to be within staggering distance of home. If you decide to DIY, again the options for a seasonal rent are better down the mountain. The Jardin Alpin shop at La Caravelle hotel in 1850 offers very low rates in hire skis for the season, just don't expect to get the latest stock.

once you're there

Where you live and/or work in the Courchevel valley will dictate what kind of season you have. 1850 has the biggest seasonnaire population (approx 600 - 1 for each ESF instructor!); 1550 the quietest seasonnaire social life. Le Praz is a mix of long-term residents (both English and French) and a handful of tour operators. La Tania is similar with fewer locals and more operators and 1650 has a nice feel. Whilst a fairly regular bus runs between the villages during the day, the last is before the bars close, so you need access to a car to enjoy what each has to offer. With so many English tour operators, the community is a little cliquey - but in a one-big-happy family way. A fair share of seasonnaires go there for the après rather than the skiing - and if that's what you want it's certainly on offer. Fads come and go so does the favourite **hangout**. That said Le Jump in 1850 is a constant. El Gringos, TJs, and the Isba in Ski World's chalet hotel seem to exist mainly for seasonnaires. With the demise of the Signal bar in 1650, the race is on to see where becomes the new in-place there. The Ski Lodge in La Tania, Darbellos in Le Praz and Le Barouf in 1550 tend to top the poles in their respective resorts. Some valley hopping goes on (again you need a car) - Wednesday night in the Rond-Point (where it's happy hour all day, all season for seasonnaires) above Méribel, Dick's Tea-Bar in Mussillon and Brewskis in St. Martin. If you have good intentions to learn something while you're there the choice includes ski lessons (NewGen runs seasonnaire-specific courses) and language lessons (French, German, Spanish, Italian) and computer courses (t 0479 083040,

i lacitedeslangues.com). For bookworms there is a library in Le Praz which has a small selection of English books.

Calls home are expensive from an English **mobile**, so it could be worth investing in a French SIM card - generally about £30 (of which £15 is call credit) and calls made within and out of France will be cheaper and you won't pay to receive calls from the UK. Check that your phone is 'unlocked' (so you can insert a foreign SIM card into it) before you leave the UK. You then pay as you go as you would in the UK. Top up cards are available from the tabacs. There is an **internet** café on Rue des Tovets and a couple of terminals in Prends ta Luge et Tire-Toi.

For full details of what's going on in and around the resort, you can tune into Radio Courchevel 93.2 FM (i radiocourchevel.com) which broadcasts information on the ski area (lifts, pistes and weather reports between 8am-9am every morning, with an English weather report at 8:45am) as well as details of events in and around the area. For less official news read the Courchevel Enquirer (i courchevelenquire.com), a seasonnaire rag. And there's always the seasonnaire grapevine. Do something outrageous, and your friends across town will likely know all about it before you even remember it yourself.

117

the a-z

tour operators

A list of the English based tour operators offering a range of accommodation in the Courchevel valley. Though many of them offer a variety of different ways to take a skiing holiday they have been categorised according to their main strength.

mainstream

airtours t 0870 238 7777,
i mytravel.com
club med t 0700 2582 932,
i clubmed.co.uk
crystal t 0870 405 5047,
i crystalski.co.uk
first choice t 0870 850 3999,
i fcski.co.uk
french life ski t 0870 197 6692,
i frenchlifeski.co.uk
inghams t 020 8780 4433,
i inghams.co.uk
leisure direction t 020 8324 4042,
i leisuredirection.co.uk
lotus supertravel t 020 7295 1650,
i supertravel.co.uk
mark warner t 0870 770 4227,
i markwarner.co.uk
neilson t 0870 333 3356,
i neilson.co.uk
thomson t 0870 606 1470,
i thomson-ski.co.uk

ski-specific

alpine action t 01273 597940, i alpine-action.co.uk
finlays t 01573 226611, i finlayski.com
french life ski t 0870 197 6692,
i frenchlifeski.co.uk
le ski t 0870 754 4444, i leski.com

on the piste travel t 01625 503 111,
i onthepiste.co.uk
pleisure t 024 7668 6835,
i pleisure.co.uk
powder white t 020 8355 8836,
i powderwhite.co.uk
silver ski t 01622 735 544,
i silverski.co.uk
simply ski t 0208 541 2209,
i simplytravel.co.uk
ski activity t 01738 840 888,
i skiactivity.co.uk
ski amis t 020 7692 0850, i skiamis.com
ski club of great britain t 020 8410 2022, i skiclub.co.uk
ski independence t 0870 600 1462,
i ski-independence.co.uk
ski olympic t 01302 328 820,
i skiolympic.co.uk
ski val t 0870 746 3000, i skival.co.uk
ski world t 08702 416723,
i skiworld.ltd.uk
snowline t 0208 870 4807,
i snowline.co.uk
total t 08701 633 633, i skitotal.com

resort-specific & independents

accommodation in the alps t 0870 136 4311, i accommodationinthealps.co.uk
alpine escape i alpine-escape.co.uk
chalet bois rond t 0474 772015
chalet le berger t 0478 436162
chalet woody wood t 0468 428071
nick ski t 0673 436769,
i nickskithreevalleys.co.uk
Qski t 01637 860 988, i Qski.net
ski n action t 01707 251 696,
i ski-n-action.com
ski dazzle t 0160 361 4498, i ski-

tour operators

dazzle.com
skideep t 0870 1645870/01483
722706/0479 081905, i skideep.com
ski fidelity t 07891 372 377,
i ski-fidelity.com
ski hame t 0187 532 0157,
i skihame.co.uk
ski magic i skimagic.co.uk
ski power t 01737 823232,
i skipower.co.uk
skivolution t 01241 874248,
i skivolution.co.uk

children

family friendly skiing t 0161 7644 520,
i familyfriendlyskiing.com
powder byrne t 020 8246 5300,
i powderbyrne.com
ski esprit t 01252 618300, i ski-
esprit.co.uk

luxury

descent t 0207 384 3854,
i descent.co.uk
elegant resorts t 01244 897 333,
i elegantresorts.co.uk
kaluma travel t 0870 4428044,
i kalumatravel.co.uk
ski scott dunn t 020 8682 5050,
i scottdunn.com
VIP t 0208 875 1957, i vip-chalets.com

self-catering & budget

ams t 01743 340623, i amsrentals.com
interhome t 020 8891 1294,
i interhome.co.uk
ski direct control t 01208 850051,
i cheapwintersports.com
skiholidays4less t 01724 290660,

i french-freedom.co.uk
into mountains i intomountains.com
ski summit i skisummit.co.uk

self-drive

drive alive t 0114 292 2971, i drive-
alive.com
erna low t 0207 584 2841,
i ernalow.co.uk
eurotunnel motoring holidays t 0870
333 2001, i eurotunnel.com

tailor-made & weekends

flexiski t 0870 9090754, i flexiski.com
made to measure holidays t 0124 353
3333, i madetomeasureholidays.com
momentum ski t 0207 371 9111,
i momentum.uk.com
ski weekend t 0870 060 0615,
i skiweekend.com
white roc ski weekends t 0207 792
1188, i whiteroc.co.uk

If you run a ski company that offers
holidays to Courchevel but are not listed
here, let us know and we'll include you
in the next edition of this guide.

directory

listings

All 04 or 06 numbers need the French international prefix (0033) if dialled from the UK. 08 numbers can only be dialled within France.

transport

air
bmibaby t 0870 264 2229,
i bmibaby.com
british airways t 0870 850 9850,
i ba.com
easyjet t 0870 600 0000,
i easyjet.co.uk
ryanair i ryanair.co.uk
swiss t 0845 601 0956, i swiss.com
chambéry t 0479 544966, i aeroport-chambery.com
geneva t 0041 22 717 7111,
i gva.ch
grenoble t 0476 654848,
i grenoble.aeroport.fr
lyon t 0826 800826, i lyon.aeroport.fr
st. etienne t 0477 557171, i saint-etienne.aeroport.fr

car hire
alamo i alamo.com
avis i avis.com (Moûtiers) t 0479 240793
easycar t 0906 333 3333
i easycar.com
europcar i europcar.com (Courchevel t 0479 240972)
hertz t 0870 844 8844 i hertz.co.uk (Moûtiers) t 0479 240775

coach travel
ski méribel t 0208 668 8223,
i skimeribel.co.uk

cross-channel
eurotunnel t 0870 535 3535,
i eurotunnel.com
norfolkline t 01304 218400,
i norfolkline.com
speedferries t 01304 203000
i speedferries.com

driving
general - carry a valid driver's licence, proof of ownership, your insurance certificate and an emergency triangle.
petrol - there is a petrol station in 1650 and in 1850 - neither is open late nor do they have 24-hour self service. It is better to fill up in Moûtiers, as higher altitude means higher prices.
signs & rules - motorways in France have blue signs. Most operate a *péage* (toll) system. You must wear a seatbelt in the front and back of a car. Children under 12 must sit in the back and babies and young children must be placed in special baby/young child seats.
speed limits - in built-up areas the speed limit is 50km/h (unless indicated). The limit is 90km/h on all other roads, 110km/h on toll-free motorways and 130km/h on toll motorways. Foreign drivers are given spot fines for speeding.
traffic info - (recorded) t 0826 022022

helicopter
(SAF) t 0479 080091, i saf-helico.com

directory

international train
raileurope t 0870 584 8848
i raileurope.co.uk
eurostar t 0870 518 6186
i eurostar.com
TGV i tgv.com

local train
SNCF t 0892 353535/ 0479 082029
i ter-sncf.com/rhone-alpes

private bus
alp line t 0677 865282, i alp-line.com
alpine cab i alpinecab.com.
ats t 0709 209 7392, i a-t-s.net
mountain transfers t 07889 942786,
i mountaintransfers.com
three vallée transfers t 01782 644 420,
i 3vt.co.uk

public bus
satobus alpes t 0472 359496, i satobus-alps.com
skibus t 0479 080117
touriscar t 0450 436002, i alpski-bus.com
transavoie t 0479 080029 (Courchevel),
0479 240423 (Moûtiers), i altibus.com
moûtiers bus station t 0479 242446

health & safety

accidents
If you have an accident on the slopes,
you will be taken to the nearest one
unless you specify a particular one. To
confirm you can pay for treatment you
will need a credit card and your
insurance details. At some point,

contact your insurance company to
check whether they want to arrange
your transport home - and ask your
doctor for a medical certificate
confirming you are fit to travel. If you
see an accident on the slopes, tell the
nearest rescue centre, usually found at
the top or bottom of lifts.

doctors
The main surgeries are in 1850 -
Cabinet Médical du Forum (t 0479
083213), Marc Chedal (t 0479 082014)
and Bernard Pépin (t 0479 082003).
The nearest hospital is in Moûtiers
(t 0479 096060) and the nearest
casualty is in Albertville.

emergency numbers
ambulances t 0479 084503
emergencies (including fire) t 18 (from
a land line), t 112 (from a mobile)
1850 fire brigade t 0479 082080
emergency medical care (SAMU) t 15
police (gendarmerie) t 17 or t 0479
082607
police municipale t 0479 083469
ski patrol 1850/1550/praz/tania
t 0479 080409, 1650 t 0479 080815

health
An E111 form (available from any UK
post office) entitles you to treatment
under the French health system. While
you have to pay for your treatment
when you receive it, you can then get a
refund for up to 70% of medical
expenses - as long as you keep all your
receipts.

directory

insurance
It is essential to have personal insurance covering wintersports and the cost of any ambulances, helicopter rescue and emergency repatriation - all these services are very expensive. Insurance policies differ greatly - some exclude off-piste skiing or cover it only if you are with a guide, so you need to check the terms and conditions carefully.

pharmacies
Either the Pharmacie Peizerat on Rue de Rocher in 1850 (t 0479 080537) or the Pharmacie Gellon on the main road in 1650 (t 0479 082617).

physiotherapists
For British physios try the British Physiotherapy Centre (t 0668 570099).

safety on the mountain
avalanche danger - the risk of avalanche is graded from 1 to 5.
1 & 2. (yellow) low risk.
3 & 4. (checked yellow and black) moderate risk, caution advised when skiing off-piste
5. (black) high risk, off-piste skiing strongly discouraged.
The risk is displayed on a flag at the main lift stations, but if you are in any doubt about where it is safe to ski, ask the advice of the lift operators.
food & drink - a skiing holiday is not the time to start a diet. Your body expends energy keeping warm and exercising so it's a good idea to eat a decent breakfast, and carry some chocolate or sweets with you. The body dehydrates more quickly at altitude and whilst exercising. You need to drink a lot (of water) each day to replace the moisture you lose.

rules of conduct - the International Ski Federation publishes conduct rules for all skiers and boarders:
1. respect - do not endanger or prejudice others.
2. control - ski in control, adapting speed and manner to ability, the conditions and the traffic.
3. choice of route - the uphill skier must choose his route so he does not endanger skiers ahead.
4. overtaking - allowed above or below, right or left, but leave enough room for the overtaken skier.
5. entering & starting a run - look up and down the piste when doing so.
6. stopping on the piste - avoid stopping in narrow places or where visibility is restricted.
7. climbing - keep to the side of the piste when climbing up or down.
8. signs & markings - respect these.
9. assistance - every skier must assist at accidents.
10. identification - all involved in an accident (including witnesses) must exchange details.

snow & avalanche information
t 0892 681020

weather
Get daily updates on t 0892 680273 (French) or online at i meteo.fr.

directory

what to wear

Several, thin layers are better than one thick piece. Avoid cotton, which keeps moisture next to the body, so cooling it down. A windproof and waterproof material (such as Goretex) is best for outer layers. A hat is essential to keep you warm and protect the scalp from sunburn as are gloves to keep hands warm. Sunglasses or goggles are essential. Wrap-arounds are a good choice and lenses should be shatter-proof and give 100% protection from UVA and UVB rays. Poor eye protection can lead to snowblindness, which makes the eyes water and feel painful and gritty. Treat by resting eyes in a darkened room, and applying cold compresses. You should wear UVA and UVB sun protection with a high factor (SPF) at all times, even if overcast and cloudy. The sun is more intense at higher altitude, so you should re-apply regularly (particularly after falling or sweating). Don't forget to cover your ear lobes and the underside of the nose.

resort survival

banks & atms

Banque de Savoie at the Croisette has a cashpoint, as does Crédit Agricole (which also has an ATM in 1650). Both are open Mondays-Fridays 8:30am-6pm (with a break for lunch) for currency exchange. CIC Lyonnaise de Banque has an ATM in 1550. There is also an ATM in Le Praz but none in La Tania.

dvds & videos

Dvds & videos can be hired from Le Cybar Café on Rue des Tovets.

internet/email

Le Cybar Café on Rue des Tovets has a number of terminals and you can sip a coffee while you surf. Prends Ta Luge et Tire-Toi in the Forum has 2 card-operated terminals.

laundry & dry cleaning

For DIY washing there is a self-service laundrette in the Forum in 1850 and in the Galerie de l'Or Blanc in Le Praz. The Blanchesserie de Moriond in 1650 will do the hard bit for you.

library

Le Praz (t 0479 010118)

lift pass company

Société des 3 Vallées t 0479 080409

newspapers

The branches of the Maison de la Presse on the first floor of the Forum and in 1650 both stock a small selection of English newspapers, as do the small newsagents in Le Praz and La Tania.

parking

Parking on the roads is allowed in the designated pay & display parking spaces - in town there are many pay & display spaces along the roads, all of which are free over lunchtime. At weekends the car parks become very busy. Do make sure that no snow clearing activity is planned (signs indicate when and where) or your car will be removed.

post

There are post offices in 1850 (t 0479 080649) at the Croisette, in 1650 (t 0479 082780) and in Le Praz (t 0479 084103) in the main commercial gallery.

radio

Radio Nostalgie (93.2 FM) broadcasts weather reports, snow conditions and resort news.

shopping

Most shops open every day (except public holidays) 8:30am-12:30pm and 2:30pm-7pm.

supermarkets - 1850 has 2 (a Sherpa in the Forum and a Casino on Rue des Tovets) and all the rest have 1 (a Sherpa), where you can stock up on the basics at some cost. If you are self-catering stop at one of the hypermarkets in Moûtiers where the range is bigger and the prices lower.

bread - good bread is easy to come by, as is good cake in 1550, 1650 and 1850 from the Boulangerie Gandy or au Pain d'Antan in 1850.

cheese - the weekly market in 1650 and 1850 always has a stall selling excellent regional produce (both cheese and cured meats).

wine - Le Baricou (t 0479 007772) and the wine shop above the Chai des Chartrons wine bar have an extensive selection of excellent vintages. For something more cheap and cheerful the

supermarkets are a better bet.

gifts - Le Lion des Sables in the Forum sells a wide enough range of confectionary and chocolate that you will find something to please your cat-sitter. For something more permanent and decorative there is a branch of the Parisian-jewellers, Agatha, as well as other diamond and gold merchants.

flowers - even Interflora has made it here - at Jasmine Fleurs on Rue de l'Eglise (t 0479 081521)

taxis

Courchevel taxis association t 0479 082346
Air Taxi t 0674 827229
Alpes Evasion taxi t 0607 696961
Altitud'taxi t 0479 081515
Arolle Taxi t 0479 010999
Gérard Blanc t 0479 084110
Locatax t 0479 011010
Premium class t 0479 000660
Eric Russo t 0608 825280
Taxi Jack t 0612 451117
Taxi Prestige des Neiges t 0479 080081
Taxi des Neiges t 0479 080883
Ecureuils Transports t 0479 080292
Taxi Roger t 0479 553103
Taxi des Cimes t 0479 083585

tourist information

1850 t 0479 080029, i courchevel.com
open Mondays-Fridays 9am-12pm, 2pm-7pm, weekends 9am-7pm
1650 t 0479 080329, 1550 t 0479 080410, le praz t 0479 084160, la tania t 0479 084040, i latania.com
open Mondays-Fridays 9am-12pm, 2pm-

directory

6pm, Saturdays 9am-12:30pm, 1:30pm-7pm.

country survival

customs
As France is part of the EU, there are few restrictions on what UK visitors can take out for personal use

electricity
220 volts/50hz ac. Appliances use a two-pin plug - adaptors are readily available from electrical stores or supermarkets.

language
English is widely spoken, though an attempt at French is widely appreciated.

money
The currency is the Euro (€). €1 is equivalent to 100 centimes. Notes come in anything from €10 to €500. You can exchange money in all the banks. In 2004, the average exchange rate for UK£1 = (approx) €1.6

public holidays
December   6 - St Nicholas Day
             25 - Christmas Day
             26 - St Stephen's day
January   1 - New Year's Day
March/April Good Friday, Easter Sunday & Monday

telephone
Public phones boxes are located throughout the town and accept coins or phonecards, which can be bought from the post office, tabacs, and train and petrol stations. All local and calls within Europe are cheaper 7pm-8am during the week and all day at the weekend. The international dialling code for France is 0033; the free international operator 12; the international directory information 1159; and national directory information 111. There are three mobile phone networks: Bouyges Telecom, France telecom/Orange and SFR.

time
France is always 1 hour ahead of England.

tipping
All food bills include a service charge, though it is common to make an addition for drinks or for noticeably good service.

water
Tap water is drinkable, except where there is an *eau non potable* sign.

glossary

a

arête - a sharp ridge.
avalanche - a rapid slide of snow down a slope.
avalanche transceiver - a device used when skiing off-piste, which can both emit and track a high frequency signal to allow skiers lost in an avalanche or a crevasse to be found.

b

BASI - British Association of Snowsport Instructors.
binding - attaches boot to ski.
black run/piste - difficult, generally steeper than a red piste.
blood wagon - a stretcher on runners used by ski patrollers to carry injured skiers off the mountain.
blue run/piste - easy, generally wide with a gentle slope.
bubble → 'gondola'.
button (or Poma) lift - for 1 person. Skis and boards run along the ground, whilst you sit on a small 'button' shaped seat.

c

cable car - a large box-shaped lift, running on a thick cable over pylons high above the ground, which carry up to 250 people per car.
carving - a recently developed turning technique used by skiers and boarders to make big, sweeping turns across the piste.
carving skis - shorter and fatter than traditional skis, used for carving turns.
chairlift - like a small and uncomfortable sofa, which scoops you and your skis off the ground and carries

you up the mountain. Once on, a protective bar with a rest for your skis holds you in place. Can carry 2-6 people.
couloir - a 'corridor' between 2 ridges, normally steep and narrow.
crampons - spiked fittings attached to outdoor or ski boots to climb mountains or walk on ice.

d

draglift or (T-bar) - for 2 people. Skis and boards run on the ground, whilst you lean against a small bar.
drop-off - a sharp increase in gradient.

e

edge - the metal ridge on the border of each side of the ski.

f

FIS - Federation Internationale du Ski.
flat light - lack of contrast caused by shadow or cloud, making it very difficult to judge depth and distance.
freeriding, freeskiing - off-piste skiing.
freestyle - skiing involving jumps.

g

glacier - a slow-moving ice mass formed thousands of years ago and fed each year by fresh snow.
gondola (or bubble) - an enclosed lift, often with seats.
green run/piste - easiest, most gentle slope.

h

heliskiing - off-piste skiing on routes only accessible by helicopter.
high season - weeks when the resort is (generally) at full capacity.

i

glossary

itinerary route (yellow) - not groomed, maintained or patrolled. Generally more difficult, at least in part, than a black piste. Can be skied without a guide.

k

kicker - jump.

l

lambchop drag ➜ 'rope tow'.
ledgy - off-piste conditions in which there are many short, sharp drop-offs.
low season - beginning and end of the season and the least popular weeks in mid-January.

m

mid season - reasonably popular weeks in which the resort is busy but not full.
mogul - a bump, small or large, on or off piste. A large mogulled area is called a mogul field.

o

off-piste - the area away from marked, prepared and patrolled pistes.

p

parallel turn - skis turn in parallel.
piste - a ski run marked, groomed and patrolled, and graded in terms of difficulty (blue, red or black).
piste basher - a bulldozer designed to groom pistes by smoothing snow.
pisteur - a ski piste patroller.
Poma ➜ 'button lift'.
powder - fresh, unbashed or untracked snow.

r

raquettes ➜ 'snowshoes'.
red run/piste - intermediate, normally steeper than a blue piste, although a

flatish piste may be a red because it is narrow, has a steep drop-off or because snow conditions are worse than on other pistes.
rope tow (or lambchop drag) - a constantly moving loop of rope with small handles to grab onto to take you up a slope.

s

schuss - a straight slope down which you can ski very fast.
seasonnaire - an individual who lives (and usually works) in a ski resort for the season.
skis - technology has changed in the last 10 years. New skis are now shorter and wider. When renting, you will be given a pair approx. 5-10cms shorter than your height.
ski patrol - a team of piste patrollers
skins - artificial fur attached to ski base, for ski touring.
snow-chains - chains attached to car tyres so that it can be driven (cautiously) over snow or ice.
snowshoes - footwear resembling tennis rackets which attach to shoes, for walking on soft snow.
spring snow - granular, heavy snow conditions common in late season (when daytime temperatures rise causing snow to thaw and re-freeze).
steeps - a slope with a very steep gradient.

t

T-bar ➜ 'draglift'.

w

white-out - complete lack of visibility caused by enveloping cloud cover.

index

index

also available...

the snowmole guides to

chamonix mont-blanc
including argentière and full
coverage of chamonix's
4 ski areas and the vallée
blanche...

la plagne paradiski
including all 10 resorts and full
coverage of the paradiski area and
the vanoise express...

les arcs paradiski
including peisey-vallandry
& arc 1950 and full coverage
of the paradiski area and the
vanoise express...

méribel les 3 vallées
including méribel centre, les
allues, méribel village & mottaret
and full coverage of the 3 vallées
ski area...

also available...

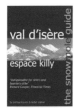

val d'isère espace killy
including st. foy and
full coverage of the espace
killy area...

verbier val de bagnes
including full coverage of the
4 vallées from verbier to
veysonnaz...

zermatt matterhorn
including full coverage of the
zermatt-cervinia ski area and the
matterhorn...

and coming soon the snowmole guides to...

st. anton arlberg
tignes espace killy
ski weekends
alpine secrets

& also the underground network

further information

accuracy & updates

We have tried our best to ensure that all the information included is accurate at the date of publication. However, because places change - improve, get worse, or even close - you may find things different when you get there. Also, everybody's experience is different and you may not agree with our opinion. You can help us, in 2 ways: by letting us know of any changes you notice and by telling us what you think - good or bad - about what we've written. If you have any comments, ideas or suggestions, please write to us at: snowmole, 45 Mysore Road, London, SW11 5RY or send an email to comments@snowmole.com

snowmole.com

Our website is intended as a compliment to our guides. Constantly evolving and frequently updated with news, you will find links to other wintersport related websites, information on our stockists and offers and the latest news about future editions and new titles. We also use our website to let you know of any major changes that occur after we publish the guides.

If you would like to receive news and updates about our books by email, please register your details at www.snowmole.com

order form

The snowmole guides are available from all major bookshops, wintersports retailers or direct from Qanuk Publishing & Design Ltd. To experience the Alps without leaving home have your next snowmole guide delivered to your door. To order send an email to sales@snowmole.com or fill in the form below and send it to us at Qanuk Publishing & Design Ltd, 45 Mysore Road, London, SW11 5RY

the snowmole guide to:	ISBN	quantity
chamonix mont blanc	0-9545739-3-5	-----------------------------
courchevel les 3 vallées	0-9545739-5-1	-----------------------------
la plagne paradiski	0-9545739-8-6	-----------------------------
les arcs paradiski	0-9545739-7-8	-----------------------------
méribel les 3 vallées	0-9545739-4-3	-----------------------------
val d'isère espace killy	0-9545739-9-4	-----------------------------
verbier val de bagnes	0-9545739-2-7	-----------------------------
zermatt matterhorn	0-9545739-6-X	-----------------------------

total: -----------------------------
(£6.99 each, postage & packaging free)

I enclose a cheque for £
(made payable to Qanuk Publishing & Design Ltd)

name --
address ---
postcode --
tel ---
email address ---
(please use block capitals)

Delivery will normally be within 14 working days. The availability and published prices quoted are correct at the time of going to press but are subject to alteration without prior notice. Please note that this service is only available in the UK.

Qanuk would like to keep you updated on new titles in the snowmole range or special offers. If you do not wish to receive such information please tick here ☐
Qanuk has a number of partners in the ski industry, and we may from time to time share your details with those partners if we think it might be of interest to you. If you do not wish us to share your details please tick here ☐

about you

Your comments, opinions and recommendations are very important to us. To help us improve the snowmole guides, please take a few minutes to complete this short questionnaire. Once completed please send it to us at Qanuk Publishing & Design Ltd.

name (Mr/Mrs/Ms) --
address --
postcode ---
email address --
age --
occupation ---

1. about your ski holiday (circle as appropriate)
how many days do you ski each year?
weekend/1 week/2 weeks/1 month/more
when do you book?
last-minute/1 month before/1-3 months before/3-6 months before/6+ months before
how do you book your holiday?
travel agent/mainstream tour operator/ski-specific tour operator/diy

2. about the snowmole guide
which title did you buy? --
where and when did you buy it? --
have you bought any other snowmole guides? -------------------------------
if so, which one(s) ---
how would you rate each section out of 5 (1 = useless, 5 = very useful)
getting started --
the skiing --
the resort --
the directory ---
the maps --
what in particular made you buy this guide? -------------------------------
----
do you have any general comments or suggestions? -------------------------
----
did you buy any other guides for your holiday? ----------------------------
if yes, which one? --
Qanuk Publishing & Design Ltd may use information about you to provide you with details of other products and services, by telephone, email or in writing. If you do not wish to receive such details please tick here ☐

about us

snowmole / snōmōl / n. & v. **1** a spy operating within alpine territory (esp. ski resorts) for the purpose of gathering local knowledge. **2** (in full **snowmole guide**) the guidebook containing information so gathered. v. research or compile or process intelligence on an alpine resort or surrounding mountainous area.

the authors
Isobel Rostron and Michael Kayson are snowsport enthusiasts who met while taking time out from real life to indulge their passion - Isobel to get it out of her system and Michael to ingrain it further. Michael's approach having won, they decided that a return to real life was overrated and came up with a cunning plan to make their passion their work. The result was snowmole.

acknowledgements & credits
None of this would have been possible without the help and support of many people:
Alexia Desnoulez (Office de Tourisme de Courchevel 1850), Zoe Bannister, Richard Lumb, Nick, Benoit & Kay Wey for their help in the resorts and Maisie, Peter & Christine Rostron, Andrew Lilley, Angela Horne, Julian Horne, Henry, Katie Fyson & Tom Fyson for their ongoing support.

The publishers would also like to thank the following for their kind permission to reproduce their photographs.
front cover: Office de Tourisme de Courchevel 1850
back cover: Office de Tourisme de Courchevel 1850 & Office de Tourisme de La Plagne
inside: title page, 10, 14, 15, 55, 82, 83, 90, 98, 104 & 108 Office de Tourisme de Courchevel 1850 and 61, 64 & 70 Office de Tourisme de Méribel
The remaining photographs are held in the publisher's own photo library and were taken by Isobel Rostron.

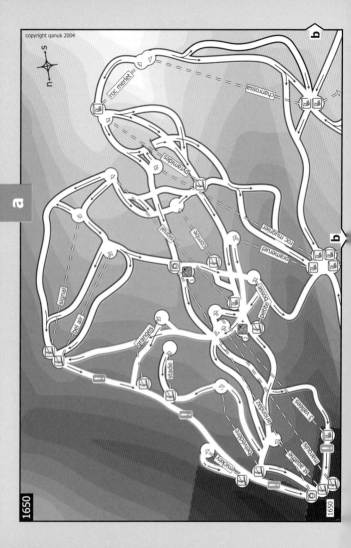

1650

1650

a

b

b

roc merlet

chanrossa

pyramides

signal

combe

roc mugnier

pramenuel

petite gosse

signal

bel air

oranges

stade

marandes

3 vallées

plan vert

st agathe

marquis

boukarde

mickey

1650

		pistes	queues	moguls	off-piste

		⏱	pistes	queues	moguls I II III IIII	off-piste I II III
st agathe	1	2m10				
marquis	1	6m40				
3 vallées	2	12m25				
ariondaz	6	13m10				
belvédère	1	3m00				
mickey	1	1m30				
stade	1	3m20				
granges	1	5m10				
bel air	1	3m50				
signal	1	7m10				
petite bosse	1	2m25				
signal	6	8m00				
combe	1	3m20				
pyramides	1x2	6m20				
prameruel	2	4m10				
roc mugnier	2	9m40				
roc merlet	3	3m50				
chanrossa	4	4m50				

1650

1 bel air
2 la casserole

prameruel/roc mugnier/ chanrossa — return from 1850 and the rest of the 3 vallées

petite bosse — use to return to 1850

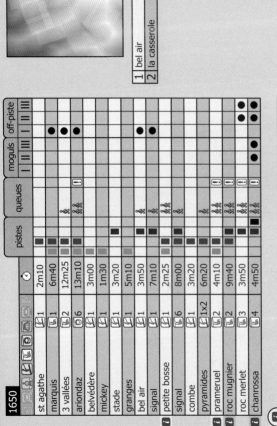

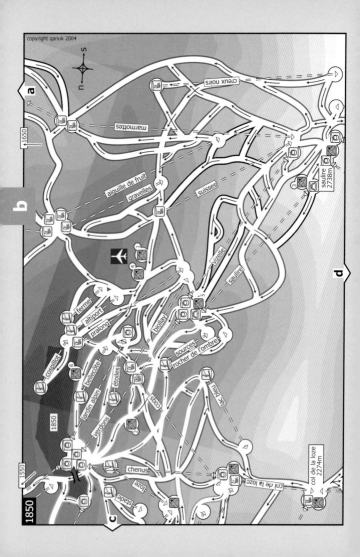

copyright qanuk 2004

1850

1650

1550

col de la loze 2274m

saulire 2738m

creux noirs

marmottes

aiguille de fruit

gravelles

suisses

vizelle

saulire

biollay

sources

rocher de l'ombre

lac bleu

ferme

altiport

pralong

cospillot

bellecôte

jardin alpin

étoiles

coqs

verdons

chenus

loze

stade

1850

	☆		pistes	queues	moguls I II III	off-piste I II III
jardin alpin	9m00	6	■ ■	⚡ ⚡ ⚡ / !		
verdons	8m40	8		⚡ ⚡ ⚡ / !		
bellecôte	4m20	1	■			
étoiles	3m20	1	■ ■			
coqs	5m30	4	■	⚡ ⚡ / !		●
cospillot	3m00	1	■	⚡		
pralong	7m30	6	■ ■	⚡		
altiport	2m30	1	■ ■			
ferme	1m30	1	■			
biollay	6m50	6	■	⚡		
sources	5m10	1	■			
rocher de l'ombre	7m00	1	■			
lac bleu	6m50	3	■			● ●
saulire	4m20	160	■ ■	⚡ ⚡ / !	●	● ●
vizelle	7m20	8	■	⚡ ⚡ / !	●	
suisses	6m40	4	■	⚡ ⚡ / !	●	●
gravelles	7m20	4				
aiguille de fruit	7m20	3	■	⚡ ⚡ / !		
marmottes	5m25	6	■	⚡ ⚡		
creux noirs	7m00	3		⚡ ⚡ / !		●

1	cap horn
2	le chalet des pierres
3	le panoramic
4	le pilatus
5	l'arc en ciel
6	la bergerie

jardin alpin — 3 stations, stays open after the pistes close for access to jardin alpin and for tobogganers

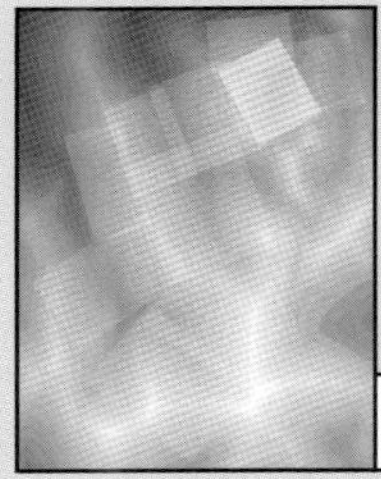

b

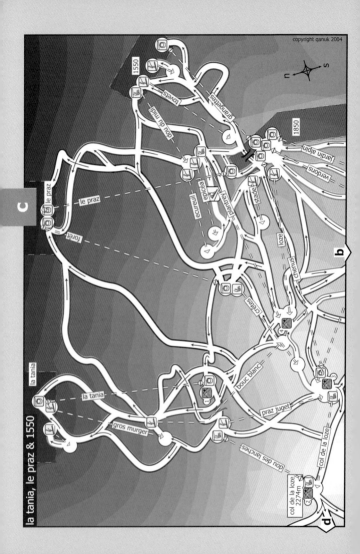

la tania, le praz & 1550

copyright qanuk 2004

col de la loze 2274m

col de la loze

dou des lanches

praz juget

bouc blanc

gros murger

la tania

la tania

1850

jardin alpin

verdons

stade

azu

chenus

crêtes

forêt

le praz

le praz

écureuil

épicéa

plantrey

tovets

dou du midi

grandes bosses

1550

la tania, le praz & 1550

la tania, le praz & 1550

		pistes	queues	moguls I / II / III	off-piste I / II / III
gros murger	7m00				
la tania	7m45			● ●	● ● ●
forêt	9m00	■	✂ !		
le praz	8m30	■	✂		
i ecureuil	3m10		✂ !		
i epicéa	3m00	■	✂		●
plantrey	7m00	■	✂ !	●	
i stade	4m00				
i dou du midi	6m20				
i tovets	7m30				
i bouc blanc	6m35				● ●
i dou des lanches	5m00	■ ■	✂ !	● ●	● ●
i col de la loze	6m45	■	✂	●	● ●
crêtes	6m05				●
i praz juget	5m00	■	✂ !	● ●	
chenus	8m55	■	✂ !		
loze	5m30	■	✂ !		●
grangettes	7m30	■ ■	✂	●	●
coqs	5m35	■ ■	✂ !		

C

i
ecureuil/epicéa	snowpark access
dou du midi/tovets	to be replaced winter 2005
col de la loze/dou des lanches	link to méribel
praz juget	téléski difficile

1 le bouc blanc
2 le roc tania
3 les chenus
4 la soucoupe

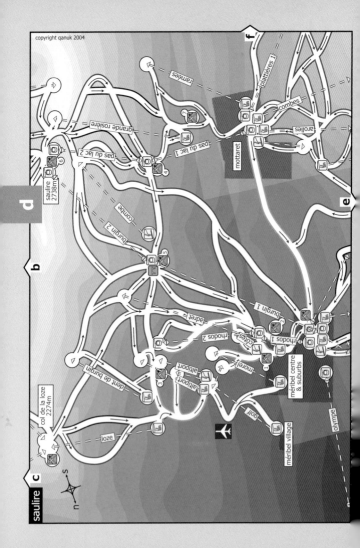

saulire

copyright qanuk 2004

saulire 2738m

col de la loze 2274m

ramées

grande rosière

pas du lac 2

pas du lac 1

combe

burgin 2

adret

burgin 1

rhodos 2

côtes

rhodos 1

morel

altiport

altiport

dent de burgin

loze

méribel centre & suburbs

méribel village

golf

olympe

mottaret

combes

arolles

plattières 1

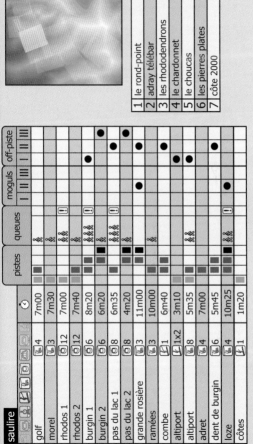

saulire

		⏱	pistes	queues	moguls I II III	off-piste I II III	
i	golf	🚠4	7m00	■	※			
i	morel	🚡3	7m30	■	※			
i	rhodos 1	🚠12	7m00	■	※ (!)			
	rhodos 2	🚠12	7m40	■	※			
i	burgin 1	🚠6	8m20	■	※ (!)		●	
	burgin 2	🚠6	6m20	■	※		●	
	pas du lac 1	🚠8	6m35	■ ■	※		●	
i	pas du lac 2	🚠8	4m20	■ ■	※ (!)		●	
	grande rosière	🚡3	11m00	■	※	●		
	ramées	🚡3	10m00					
i	combe	🚡1	6m40	■			●	
	altiport	🚡1x2	3m10				● ●	
	altiport	🚠8	5m35	■	※		●	
	adret	🚡4	7m00	■				
	dent de burgin	🚠6	5m45	■	※		●	
	loze	🚠4	10m25	■	※ (!)			
	côtes	🚡1	1m20	■				

i legend:

i	golf	link from méribel village
	morel	link from the lower suburbs
	rhodos 1	link to le rond-point
	burgin 2/pas du lac 2	courchevel valley access
	combe	téléski difficile

1 le rond-point
2 adray télébar
3 les rhododendrons
4 le chardonnet
5 le choucas
6 les pierres plates
7 côte 2000

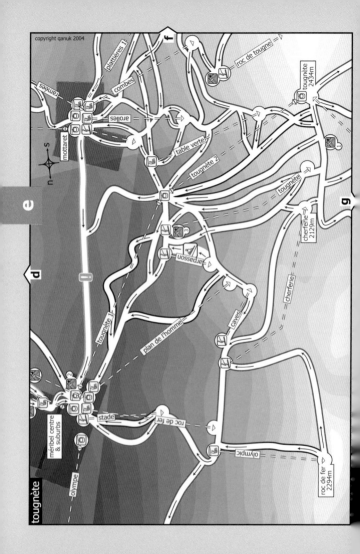

tougnète

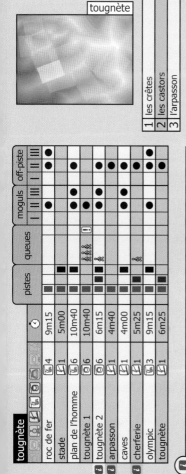

tougnète

1	les crêtes
2	les castors
3	l'arpasson

tougnète		pistes	queues	moguls I II III IIII	off-piste I II III IIII
roc de fer	9m15			●	●
stade	5m00				
plan de l'homme	10m40			●	●
tougnète 1	10m40		1	● ●	●
tougnète 2	6m15		⋘	●	●
arpasson	4m40		⋘	●	●
caves	4m00				●
cherferie	5m25		⋘	●	●
olympic	9m15			●	●
tougnète	6m25				●

tougnète 2 — links to st. martin & belleville valley, often closed in high winds

arpasson — snowpark access

cherferie — téléski difficile

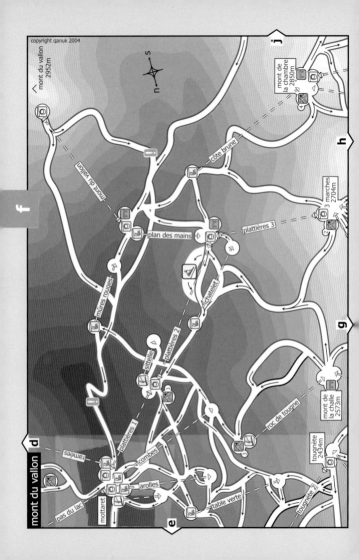

mont du vallon

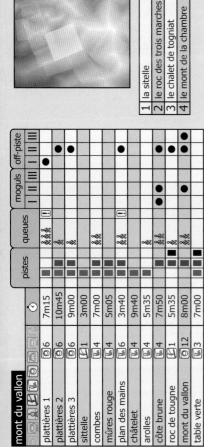

mont du vallon

		la sitelle
1		la sitelle
2		le roc des trois marches
3		le chalet de togniat
4		le mont de la chambre

		⏱	pistes	queues	moguls I	moguls II	moguls III	off-piste I	off-piste II	off-piste III
plattières 1	6	7m15		⚞ (!)					●	
plattières 2	6	10m45		⚞⚞						●
plattières 3	6	9m00		⚞						●
sitelle	1	3m00								
combes	4	7m00		⚞⚞						
mûres rouge	4	5m05		⚞⚞					●	
plan des mains	6	3m40		⚞⚞ (!)						
châtelet	4	9m40								
arolles	4	5m35		⚞		●			●	
côte brune	4	7m50		⚞⚞		●			●	
roc de tougne	1	5m35		⚞						●
mont du vallon	12	8m00		⚞⚞		●				●
table verte	3	7m00								

ⓘ

plattières 2	exit at the top of plattières 2 to reach the côte brune chair and the link to val thorens
plattières 3	st. martin/les menuires access
mûres rouge	use to reach the plan des mains chair and avoid the 'ours' piste
plan des mains	return from val thorens/les menuires
arolles	use to reach mottaret accommodation at the end of the day
côte brune	val thorens access, often closed in high winds
mont du vallon	closes in high winds

f

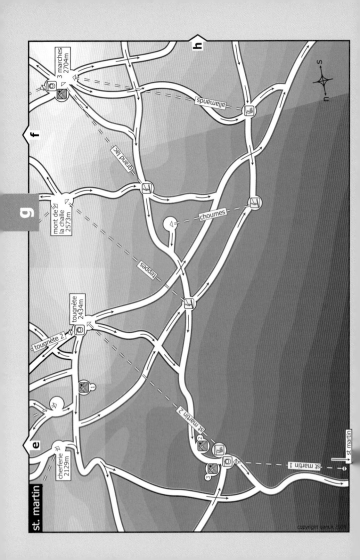

st. martin

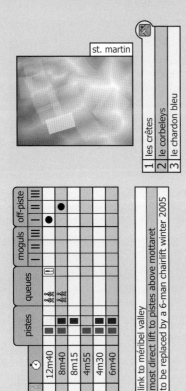

st. martin

		⏱	pistes	queues	moguls I II III	off-piste I II III
st. martin 1	🚡8	12m40			●	
st. martin 2	🚠4	8m40		≋≋		●
teppes	🚏1	8m15	■	≋≋		
choumes	🚏1	4m55	■			
grand lac	🚏1	4m30	■			
allamands	🚏3	6m40	■			

ⓘ st. martin 2 — link to méribel valley
teppes — most direct lift to pistes above mottaret
choumes/grand lac — to be replaced by a 6-man chairlift winter 2005

1 les crêtes
2 le corbeleys
3 le chardon bleu

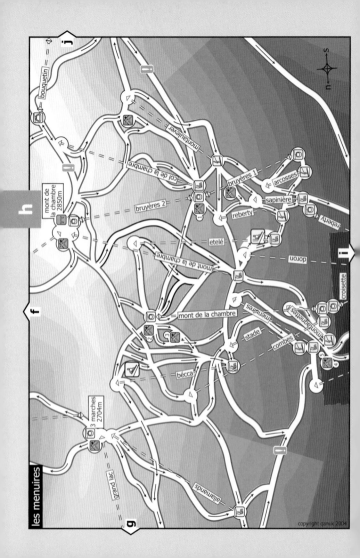

les menuires

1 les quatre vents
2 le chalet du cairn
3 le chalet des neiges
4 le chalet de capricorne
5 sphère

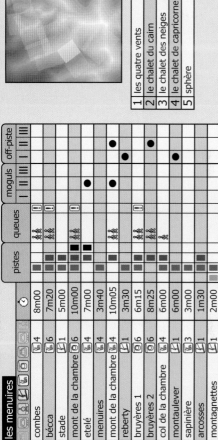

les menuires

		⏱	pistes	queues	moguls I	II	III	off-piste I	II	III
combes	4	8m00								
bécca	6	7m20		⚅						
stade	1	5m00								
mont de la chambre	6	10m00		⚅						
etelé	4	7m00								
menuires	4	3m40			•					
mont de la chambre	4	10m05			•			•		
reberty	1	3m30								
bruyères 1	6	6m15		⚅						
bruyères 2	6	8m25						•		
col de la chambre	4	6m00						•		
montaulever	1	6m00								
sapinière	3	3m00								
arcosses	1	1m30								
montagnettes	1	2m00								

ℹ bécca — return to the méribel valley by the roc des 3 marches

mont de la chambre/ bruyères 2/col de la chambre — return to the méribel valley by the mont de la chambre

h

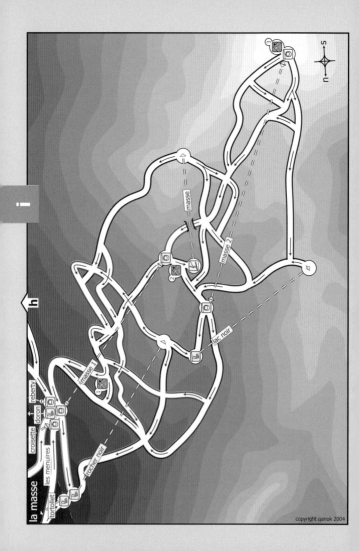

la masse

tortollet
les menuires
croisette
doron
reberty
rocher noir
masse 1
masse
masse 2
lac noir

copyright qanuk 2004

la masse

la masse

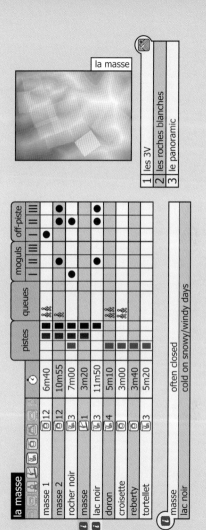

	🕐	pistes	queues	moguls I II III	off-piste I II III
masse 1	12	6m40	■■ ≋		
masse 2	12	10m55	■■ ≋	●	● ●
rocher noir	3	7m00	■■		●
masse	1	3m20	■ ■	●	
lac noir	3	11m50	■		● ●
doron	4	5m10	■		
croisette	0	3m00	■ ≋	●	
reberty	0	3m40	■ ≋		
tortellet	3	5m20			

masse — often closed
lac noir — cold on snowy/windy days

1 les 3V
2 les roches blanches
3 le panoramic

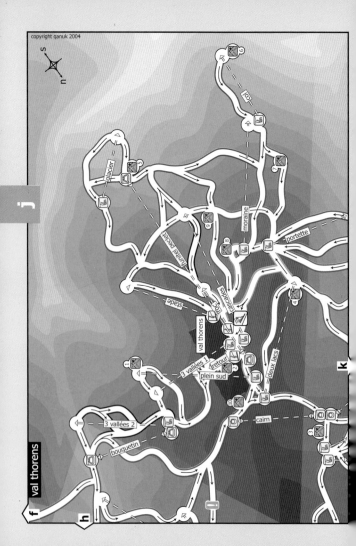

copyright qanuk 2004

val thorens

glacier

stade

tunnel peclet

cascades

moraine

portette

val thorens

3 vallées 1

retour

plein sud

deux lacs

3 vallées 2

bouquetin

cairn

f

h

j

k